The
Vegetarian
Low-Carb Diet
Cookbook

A note on stevia

Stevia is a natural sweetener that can be used as an alternative to sugar. Made from a herb, it is extremely concentrated: a speck of pure stevia the size of a sesame seed is equivalent to a teaspoonful of sugar. Stevia has been shown to have a regulating effect on the pancreas. It also helps stabilise blood sugar levels, acts as a general tonic, reduces stomach acid and gas, and inhibits the bacteria that cause dental decay and gum disease.

Stevia in the UK

At the time of writing, it is illegal to sell stevia in the UK. Stevia is available in the US, Canada, Australia and New Zealand. It is possible to purchase stevia on the internet and have it sent to UK addresses.

Recipes that have a **V** symbol are suitable for vegans.

The Vegetarian Low-Carb Diet Cookbook

The fast, no-hunger weightloss cookbook for vegetarians

Rose Elliot

PIATKUS

Visit the Piatkus website!

Piatkus publishes a wide range of best-selling fiction and non-fiction, including books on health, mind, body & spirit, sex, self-help, cookery, biography and the paranormal.

If you want to:

- read descriptions of our popular titles
- buy our books over the internet
- take advantage of our special offers
- enter our monthly competition
- learn more about your favourite Piatkus authors

VISIT OUR WEBSITE AT: **www.piatkus.co.uk**

First published in Great Britain in 2006 by
Piatkus Books Ltd
5 Windmill Street, London W1T 2JA
email: info@piatkus.co.uk

A catalogue record for this book is available from the British Library

ISBN 0 7499 2698 8

Edited by Jan Cutler
Design and typesetting by Paul Saunders

Some of the recipes appearing in this book have been adapted from original recipes in *Vegetarian Four Seasons*.

This book has been printed on paper manufactured with respect for the environment using wood from managed sustainable resources

Printed and bound in Great Britain at the Bath Press, Somerset

contents

acknowledgements   vi

introduction   1

the vegetarian low-carb diet: what it is,
   why it works and how to do it   3

the low-carb kitchen:
   equipment and storecupboard   13

drinks, shakes and smoothies   22

hot and cold breakfasts   29

soups   38

salads   45

sauces, salsas and dressings   59

dips and dippers   70

fried, braised and grilled meals   80

curries, casseroles and stir-fries   92

'pasta' dishes   101

bakes   109

side vegetables   122

hot and cold desserts   130

bread and baked treats   143

sources and stockists   150

index   152

To the four 'C's who have all inspired,
encouraged and helped me – thank you!

acknowledgements

First of all I would like to thank everyone who bought *The Vegetarian Low-Carb Diet*; you bought the book, you lost the weight, and you asked for more recipes – so here they are! Also I would like to thank my lovely publisher, Judy Piatkus, and Gill Bailey, for making it possible, and Jo Brooks, Jan Cutler and Paul Saunders for all their work on the editing and design and to my agent, Barbara Levy for all her usual wise advice and help and Anna for nutritional advice. I would also like to thank Jane Donovan and Helen Stanton for their work on the proofreading.

I would like to say a very special thank you to my enormously organised and talented daughter Claire, whose assistance both in the kitchen and editorially enabled me to meet the deadline, and to my dear husband Robert, unfailingly patient and supportive as usual though by no means a 'low-carber'. To the rest of my family and friends I would also like to say thank you for your understanding and thoughtfulness.

introduction

I first became interested in the low-carb diet when, at the height of the Atkins fervour, I was forever reading about vegetarian celebrities 'defecting' to meat eating in order to lose weight. At the same time there was a great deal of emphasis on the amount of meat that these dieters were eating. The general assumption was that it was impossible, or even dangerous, for a vegetarian (or even worse, a vegan!) to attempt a low-carb way of eating. I really couldn't see why this should be the case and was intrigued by this new approach to weightloss. Eager to set the record straight as far as vegetarianism was concerned, I looked into the diets further.

So, for all of these reasons I researched the subject thoroughly, with the help and advice of a state-registered dietician, and also successfully tried the diet myself. I found that the vegetarian (and vegan) versions did indeed work, and work extremely well. Many successful dieters, some of whom had lost many, many pounds, were kind enough to share their experiences and the secrets of their success. The result was my book, *The Vegetarian Low-Carb Diet*, which explains the diet in detail and includes my recipes for healthy and enjoyable low-carb eating.

Since then, despite what you might have read in the press about low-carb dieting being 'over', interest, certainly in the vegetarian version, has continued to grow, hence this new cookbook, which introduces a feast of new recipes.

The reason why low-carb eating and dieting continue to flourish is, primarily, that they work! This is because when you reduce your carbohydrates substantially your body switches to fat-burning mode. There is no more glucose to burn as energy so fat is burned instead. You also feel full and satisfied and do not get 'cravings'.

People like the diet because it enables them to lose weight, encouragingly fast at first, then steadily, and it can then be tailored to maintain a healthy weight. They also like the diet because they don't feel hungry between meals and because they feel so good on it. In fact, one of the things I notice most when talking to those who are following the vegetarian low-carb diet is the number of people who comment on how well they feel. Of course, no one would claim that it's a panacea for all ills, but time and again I hear the same thing. Once they get past the first few days of adjustment, low-carbers say how well they feel, how much more energy they have, how much better they sleep at night, how much stronger their nails and hair have become, and so on.

The vegetarian diet is known to be an essentially healthy way of eating. Focusing a little more on the protein content, eating nuts and healthy oils, as well as plenty of vegetables, as advocated in this diet, seems to make it even more so. The abundance of vegetables is also one advantage which the vegetarian low-carb diet has over the meat version: to do the vegetarian low-carb diet you *have* to eat a lot of vegetables, and many green ones at that, which makes this a particularly healthy way to low-carb.

Another reason why people get on well with this diet is, quite simply, the food. It's delicious, tasty, filling and satisfying. And, surprisingly, it's not antisocial in the way some diets are; it's quite easy for a low-carb vegetarian to eat out, and to eat with friends. Although it's not quite so easy for a vegan, I'll admit, but delicious tofu dishes are definitely becoming more common as is the number of low-carb vegan meat substitutes, many of which are based on TVP (textured vegetable protein). It is also becoming easier to find restaurants serving adventurous food made with these ingredients.

Being able to eat with other people, and to enjoy plenty of variety, are undoubtedly two of the secrets of long-term success with a diet, and they are the reason for this new book. Having lost weight on the vegetarian low-carb diet and enjoyed the meals, people are asking for second helpings!

This book begins with a concise overview of the diet – what it is, why it works and how to do it, in a nutshell. This is followed by a list of the ingredients that you will need to follow the diet, what they are, where to get them and tips for using them. The recipes that follow are grouped together so that you can easily plan your day ahead, and each one includes carb and protein counts.

Whether you are an experienced vegetarian low-carber, or just starting out on the diet – or, indeed, someone looking for recipes that taste good and are easy to make – I hope you will enjoy reading and using this book and will find it a useful companion volume to *The Vegetarian Low-Carb Diet*.

the vegetarian low-carb diet:
what it is, why it works and how to do it

If you want to lose weight fast, get to know the essentials of the diet first and then choose your complete day's menu from the recipe section. Each recipe gives you the important information you need to know so that you can easily slot it into a strict or not-too-strict low-carb diet. Of course, the recipes can also stand alone as a delicious and healthy addition to *any* diet.

what it is

The vegetarian low-carb diet is a fast, effective, healthy and enjoyable way of losing weight, which many people find easy to stick to because the food is so delicious.

The basic principles are simple:

- Reduce carbohydrates (carbs)
- Boost protein
- Eat healthy fats

There's plenty of proof that it works. In comparative trials, people on the low-carb diet lost weight faster in the first six months than those on other diets, particularly low-fat diets. After that, the groups evened up, with weightloss continuing at the rate of about 0.5–1kg (1–2lb) a week.

Along with the weightloss came many positive benefits:

- Lowered blood pressure and cholesterol levels
- Better blood-glucose control, meaning more stable blood sugar levels and fewer mood swings
- Better insulin sensitivity

not so newfangled

Because of its recent surge in popularity, people tend to think of the low-carb diet as something very new. In fact, this diet has been around for well over a century.

The first ever recorded slimmer, William Banting, did it as long ago as the early 1860s. He lost nearly 0.5kg (1lb) a week for a year and transformed his health on a diet 'from which bread, cereals and starchy food were excluded' and went on to write the first diet book about it.

It amuses me to remember that this is exactly what my parents did in the 1960s when they wanted to lose weight. They didn't count carbs – they didn't even talk about carbs. They simply cut out what they called 'starch' and 'sugar' from their diets – bread, potatoes, rice, biscuits, cakes, and so on – and just ate protein (in their case, veggie protein) with lots of non-starchy vegetables, and fresh fruit for dessert, and it worked a treat. So there's nothing new under the sun ...

why it works

When you reduce the amount of carbohydrates you are eating – particularly sugar, flour products, refined grains and potatoes – and increase the amount of protein, instead of burning the sugars in carbohydrates for fuel, it burns your fat stores. It's as simple as that. You therefore lose weight quickly, because:

- You're burning fat stores
- Protein and fat fill you up so you feel satisfied for longer
- The food is good so you don't feel deprived while losing weight – and keeping it off

what's bad about carbs?

The trouble with most carbs is that they get broken down into sugars so fast, and that in our modern lifestyle we eat so many of them, especially refined carbs such as sugar and white flour in pasta and cakes.

Our body breaks them down quickly, they enter our bloodstream and we get a sugar 'high'. Insulin is released to clear the sugar away quickly (for immediate energy or to be stored as fat). Then we get an energy slump, may feel empty and hungry, and eat more carbs to lift us up again, and so the cycle goes on.

Over time, the body becomes resistant to insulin, so more and more is needed to remove the sugar from our bloodstream. Too much insulin leads to weight gain, chronic tiredness, headaches and even, eventually, to diabetes.

how the low-carb diet helps

The low-carb diet can lift us out of this cycle. When we restrict carbs, we don't get the sugar highs and lows. As our levels of insulin decrease, the 'good' hormone, glycogen, which works in balance with insulin, increases.

Glycogen has the opposite effect to insulin: instead of making the body store fat, it makes it burn it, so the weight drops off.

Glycogen also lowers cholesterol because it takes it out of the blood circulation instead of depositing it, so that's another plus.

low-carb v 'high protein'

It is important to know that the vegetarian low-carb diet is *not* 'high protein'. The amount of protein on which it is based – 60–80g (2¼–2¾oz) a day – is in fact what dieticians call 'adequate'.

It is true that *high* protein diets have been associated with a risk of kidney damage *in people who already have a kidney problem and don't realise it* (which can happen with diabetics). However, because this is *not* a high protein diet the risk of kidney damage is not a problem. But if you have any worries about your health, do of course consult your doctor before following the diet – as indeed it is wise before embarking on any diet, and I do recommend this.

It's even possible that the vegetarian low-carb diet might actually be good for your kidneys. Studies have shown that eating soya protein, which features strongly in this diet, may have a protective effect on them.

The vegetarian low-carb diet will not weaken your bones, either. Certainly, you'll lose a little more calcium than usual at the very beginning of the diet, when you're losing excess water, but this happens on any diet. After that your calcium balance will return to normal with no long-term damage.

shouldn't we worry about eating fat?

Yes, we should worry about eating *enough* of the *right* fats. Most of us are eating too many of the *wrong* kind of fats and are starved of the healthy ones. The vegetarian low-carb diet with its emphasis on olive oil, nuts, seeds, avocados and eggs puts this right.

As far as cholesterol in the blood is concerned, this is influenced by a number of factors including the amount of insulin our bodies are producing, not just the amount of fat we eat. Reducing the amount of insulin our bodies produce, by restricting our carbs, also lowers cholesterol, as I've explained above. (The health aspects of the low-carb diet are fully described in my book, *The Vegetarian Low-Carb Diet*.)

How to do it

The vegetarian low-carb diet has three phases:

Phase 1 This is the **Carb Cleanse**, when carbs are cut to 20g (¾oz) a day. It gets your metabolism working and results in an encouraging weightloss. Most people start the diet with this phase. It is usually followed for a fortnight but can be longer if you are finding it effective, feeling good and want to continue.

Phase 2 During this **Continued Weightloss** phase you gradually increase your daily carbs week by week to anything up to about 60g (2¼oz) a day until your weightloss stabilises at about 0.5–1kg (1–2lb) per week. However, most people find that increasing their carbs by around 45–50g (about 1¾oz) gives the best results. Some people choose to skip Phase 1 and start at this higher carb level, which allows a much wider range of foods with plenty of scope for interesting and delicious meals.

Phase 3 During this **Maintenance** phase you will be able to increase your carbs yet again to a level that keeps your weight steady, and you will be able to add an even greater variety of ingredients to your diet, as well as reintroducing some old favourite foods if you want to. The amount of carbs will vary according to your own metabolism; they could be as low as 50g (about 1¾oz) per day or as high as 150g (5½oz).

you can choose how 'strict' you want to be

If you start the diet with Phase 1, on the lowest number of carbs – 20g (¾oz) per day – you will kick-start your metabolism, making it burn fat instead of glucose, and you will lose weight extra-quickly.

This fat-burning mode is called ketosis and usually starts 48 hours after cutting carbs right back. As long as you are getting plenty of calories from protein and fat (and not starving yourself), ketosis simply shows you that your body is burning fat. (Yippee!) This is fine; in fact, it's a plus, because most people feel wonderful when they are in ketosis once they have adjusted to it: clear-headed and energetic, with no carb cravings. Ketosis is also a natural appetite suppressant – and what dieter wouldn't want that? Bad breath, a common problem for people following the meat-based, low-carb diets, does not seem to be a particular problem for people on a vegetarian low-carb diet.

Just remember to eat regularly and to get enough calories and fat to make the process work safely and effectively. Because all the recipes in the book give carb and protein counts, it is easy to calculate your carb intake effortlessly each day.

if you choose to be more relaxed …

Taking it nice and easy and starting the diet at a level of carbs above 20g (¾oz) per day means that you probably won't experience ketosis, but you will still lose weight steadily and successfully. Indeed, there are several well-known and successful low-carb diets that start at this higher level and they achieve excellent long-term results.

cutting (and counting) carbs

As I've explained above, to follow the vegetarian low-carb diet successfully, it is important to follow three simple principles: cut carbohydrates (carbs), boost protein and eat healthy fats. So, as with any diet, you do have to keep track of what you are eating – and, yes, you do have to COUNT YOUR CARBS! But this is not difficult.

Counting your carbs

Simply make a note of what you have eaten, choosing recipes that fit in with the carb level you have chosen (Phase 1: no more than 20g (¾oz) a day; Phase 2: up to 45–50g (about 1¾oz) or even 60g (2¼oz) a day; or Phase 3: to a level that maintains your weight). The best way to count your carbs is to use the Carb and Protein Counter found in *The Vegetarian Low-Carb Diet*. You'll get used to counting carbs so quickly that soon it will become second nature. Alternatively, you can use the carb and protein counter on one of the US websites I have listed on page 151.

To make it simple: all the recipes in this book include carb and protein counts.

The majority of labels on bought foods give you the number of carbs they contain. One thing you need to know is that sometimes the carbs given on the label include the fibre, too, but as fibre has no effect on insulin levels, fibre carbs don't have to be included. You can simply subtract the grams of fibre from the total carbs stated.

So, if the label on a packet states that the food contains 12g carbohydrates and 7g fibre, you simply subtract the fibre from the carbohydrates (12 – 7 = 5) to find out how many carbs you need to count: in this case 5g. These are called 'net carbs', or the 'effective carbohydrate content' (ECC) or 'usable carbs'.

Sometimes packets can be confusing and state a carb total that has already had the fibre taken off. So when you subtract the fibre you get a 'too good to be true' total, or even a negative total. A negative total (a minus number) is never correct.

Don't worry, if in doubt you can usually double-check from a carb counter in a book or on the internet (see Sources and Stockists pages 150–1). In any case you'll soon get a feeling for the amount of carbs a product is likely to contain.

All the carb counts in this book have had the fibre subtracted.

carbs in fruit and vegetables

All fruit and vegetables contain some carbs, but many of them are very low. In my experience, most successful vegetarian low-carbers find they can eat large amounts of vegetables – and also berries and other low-carb fruits – once they have got past the first stages of the diet (or straight away, if they are starting at Phase 2), as long as they avoid the very starchy ones such as potatoes. As a benchmark it is interesting to know that a medium apple has 12g of carbs so perhaps they are best left for when you have reached your target weight. Pulses, the old favourite for vegetarians, are also too high in carbs for the early phases, but, again, you can reintroduce them gently when you have reached your target weight.

Remember, when calculating your carbs:

For **Phase 1**, **Carb Cleanse**, eat no more than 20g (¾oz) total carbs per day.

For **Phase 2**, **Continued Weightloss**, eat no more than 60g (2¼oz) total carbs per day (or 45–50g (about 1¾oz) for the best results).

For **Phase 3**, **Maintenance**, the total amount of carbs that keeps your weight level.

Low-carb vegetables

Carbs given are for 100g (3½oz), listed in ascending order:

Endive	0.6g	Asparagus	1.8g
Chinese leaves	0.6g	Bamboo shoots, canned	1.8g
Bean sprouts	0.7g	Radishes	1.8g
Watercress	0.7g	Mushrooms, white/button	2g
Chicory	0.9g	Baby sweetcorn	2g
Daikon	1.2g	Rocket	2.1g
Sweet Romaine lettuce	1.2g	Swiss chard	2.1g
Bok choy/Pak choi	1.2g	Courgettes	2.3g
Spinach, chopped frozen	1.2g	Tomatoes	2.7g
Spinach leaves	1.4g	Salsify	2.8g
Celery	1.4g	Green peppers	2.9g

Cabbage	3g	Spring onions	4.7g
Cucumber	3.1g	Mangetouts	5g
Cauliflower	3.3g	Spaghetti squash	5.1g
Portobello (field) mushrooms	3.6g	Artichokes (globe)	5.8g
Green beans	3.7g	Pumpkin	6g
Okra	3.8g	Aubergine	6.2g
Broccoli	4g	Onions	8.7g
Red pepper	4g	Butternut squash	9.7g
Fennel bulb	4.2g	Water chestnuts (canned)	9.8g
Turnips	4.6g	Leeks	12.4g

Low-carb fruit

Carbs given are for 100g (3½oz), listed in ascending order:

Rhubarb, canned unsweetened	1g	Watermelon	7.2g
Blackberries	4.3g	Cantaloupe melon	7.3g
Frozen mixed fruits (check pack)	5.4g	Loganberries	7.9g
Raspberries	5.5g	Honeydew melon	8.3g
Strawberries	5.7g	Peach	9g
Gooseberries	5.9g	Orange	10g

boosting protein

Remember, protein is what keeps you full, staves off hunger and keeps your energy up, so make sure you eat enough. A woman needs around 60g (2¼oz) of protein a day, a man around 80g (2¾oz). This, as I have said before, is what dieticians consider 'adequate protein'. So, in the vegetarian low-carb diet we're talking about spreading 60–80g (2¼–2¾oz) of protein throughout the day, for an expenditure of 20–60g (¾–2¼oz) or more carbs, depending on the stage of the diet you are at. This works out at 20–27g (about ¾oz) protein per meal, or 15–20g (about ½oz) per meal plus one or two protein snacks totalling 15–20g (about ½oz).

Unlike meat and fish, virtually all vegetarian proteins also contain some carbs, which have to be included in the day's total. Here are some examples of vegetarian proteins:

Carbs and protein in vegetarian protein foods

Protein and carbs given are for a portion size.

	protein	carbs
250g (9oz) firm tofu	40g	2.5g
vegeburger 'quarterpounder'	27g	1.8g
28g (1oz) or 1 scoop soya protein isolate powder	24g	0g
70g (2½oz) 'serving' wheat protein (seitan)	19g	2.5g
1 scoop microfiltered whey powder	16g	1g
2 vegetarian sausages	15g	1.8g
55g (2oz) Cheddar cheese	14g	0.4g
2 eggs	12g	1g
87g (3oz) 'serving' of Quorn chunks	12g	5g
300ml (½ pint) unsweetened soya milk	11g	1.2g
28g (1oz) pumpkin seeds	7g	4g
28g (1oz) sunflower seeds	6.5g	2.3g
28g (1oz) almonds	6g	2.3g
28g (1oz) flax (linseed)	5.5g	1.8g
28g (1oz) sesame seeds	5g	3.3g
1 tablespoon peanut butter	4.5g	2g
tahini, 15g (1 tablespoon)	4.4g	1.2g
28g (1oz) walnuts	4.3g	2g
28g (1oz) brazil nuts	4g	1.4g
28g (1oz) pinenuts	3.9g	2.7g
28g (1oz) pecan nuts	2.6g	1.4 g
28g (1oz) macadamia nuts	2.2g	1.2g

As you can see, there are lots of proteins you can eat – you just have to choose them carefully, and always check the packet when buying 'convenience' foods. The number of high-protein, low-carb vegetarian foods available is increasing. And if you're following the recipes in this book, most of which are high in protein, you will get enough anyway without really trying, while enjoying some wonderful meals.

adding fat

When you cut back on carbs, you must make sure you are getting enough fat. And as vegetables and most vegetarian proteins aren't very fatty, this means adding good-quality fats and oils to your meals. Use organic and cold-pressed olive oil, flaxseed oil and coconut oil. A little butter and cream is fine, too; choose organic if possible. Eat some cheese and all the eggs you want.

You can have crunchy salads with lovely vinaigrette or mayonnaise, buttery omelettes, crisply fried tofu, stir-fried vegetables, asparagus with hollandaise sauce, cheese melted over courgettes, sweet berries with cream – the list goes on. Have a look at the recipes and you'll get the idea.

The recipes are intended to be tempting and varied, enabling you to feel increasingly healthy while losing weight if you need to. Just follow these guidelines and enjoy the mouth-watering meals.

which drinks?

The best drink when you are low-carbing, especially if you're following it to lose weight, is water, pure and simple. Some carb-free flavoured waters can give variety, but fruit juice is too high in carbs (unless very well diluted) and diet drinks tend to be sweetened with aspartame, which in my opinion is not a desirable sweetener to have regularly and can impede weightloss. Tea is fine, as are unsweetened herbal teas (as long as they do not contain actual pieces of fruit). Cocoa can be used with cream or soya milk to make a chocolate drink (it contains a carb or two, which need to be counted). Coffee has 1g carb per cup and, strictly speaking, should be counted when you start the diet, although once you are into the later stages you needn't bother too much about the odd carb here and there. Remember to add on the extra carbs if you have any drink with milk, cream or sugar. According to some experts, wine is acceptable but opinions vary as to its carb-count; I recommend erring on the side of caution and allowing 5g a glass.

the low-carb kitchen:
equipment and storecupboard

equipment

To prepare and cook fabulous low-carb recipes, you don't need lots of expensive or fancy equipment, although there are a few items that are helpful for making quick and simple meals.

A STICK BLENDER

I really wouldn't want to be without this useful piece of equipment for any type of cookery. It is perfect for making smoothies and dips, not to mention the dressings, soups and sauces that are such a delicious part of low-carb cooking – it's a joy to use. You could use a blender or food processor instead, but a stick blender is particularly handy as you can use it directly in the saucepan or bowl, as well as in the goblet provided.

AN ELECTRIC COFFEE GRINDER

Useful for grinding almonds and flax seeds, which are frequently used in vegetarian low-carb cooking. I use mine for grinding spices as well; it's much quicker and easier than using a pestle and mortar.

ACCURATE ELECTRONIC SCALES

These are useful if you are planning to follow the diet and keep track of your carbs carefully, although they are by no means essential for general low-carb cooking. You don't need to buy very sophisticated scales; I use the cheapest type, which just give the weight in either metric or imperial.

BAKING PARCHMENT

I use this so much in my recipes that I thought I would list it here so that you can be prepared. You can buy it in any supermarket. I think it's a fantastic invention: use it to line baking sheets, and nothing will stick to them; line cake tins with it, and you don't have to grease them as well.

REFRIGERATOR SPACE

No, I'm not suggesting you go out and buy a new one, but I'm just giving you advance warning to clear plenty of space for the fresh ingredients you will be using. The more fresh vegetables you can keep in the refrigerator, the less frequently you will have to shop. In my experience you can never have too much refrigerator space.

storecupboard

Most of the ingredients used in low-carb vegetarian cookery, and in this book, are straightforward ones that you would probably buy anyway. Although you may need to go to a specialist shop or send away for one or two of the more unusual ones used in a few of the recipes, you can usually find a substitute. You will find details of where to get these less usual items under Sources and Stockists (pages 150–1).

proteins

EGGS

I always use free-range eggs, and preferably organic.

CHEESE

You can eat any cheeses that are suitable for vegetarians. The carbs are usually very low, but always double-check, and avoid cheeses with fruit in them (such as apricot or cranberries), as these will increase the carb value. If you are buying cheese from the deli counter, you may find that the assistants are able to look up the necessary information for you in the details they keep; many cheeses are vegetarian, for example, although they may not be marked as such. Vegan cheeses are higher in carbs than dairy cheeses, although some are low enough for the diet. Read the labels to check.

YOGURT

Plain, unsweetened, dairy or soya yogurt is suitable. Real 'live' yogurt is best (but check the label carefully), because you need only to count half the carbs stated on the pack. This is because the live bacteria will have eaten some of the carbs (bless 'em!). Apart from being delicious, whole-milk or Greek yogurt is best for this diet because it's lower in carbs. Look out, too, for Sojasun, a fabulous French soya yogurt – or 'soya speciality', as it says on the label – which you can find in good health and organic shops.

NUTS

Most nuts are low in carbs and offer useful amounts of protein. Almonds are particularly good, and ground almonds are frequently used in the recipes as a flour replacement. It's best to buy whole almonds (not blanched) and to grind them yourself, including their skins, to a powder in an electric coffee grinder. (The brown skins raise the fibre content and therefore lower the carbs.) You can, however, use ready-ground almonds; these are a little higher in carbs (but not much) because they don't contain the brown skins. Other useful nuts are brazil nuts, walnuts, pecan nuts, peanuts, macadamia nuts, pine nuts and hazel nuts.

NUT BUTTERS

Peanut and almond butters are especially good. Try to get organic ones without emulsifiers. The oil and solids will separate in the jar, but all you need to do is give the butter in the jar a stir.

SEEDS

Flax (linseeds), pumpkin, sesame and sunflower seeds are all low or fairly low in carbs. Flax seeds are particularly useful, being high in protein, low in carbs and rich in omega-3 oil. In fact, flax seeds are one of the best sources of omega-3 on the planet, and they are a 'must' for any vegetarian or vegan (or anyone at all), whether low-carbing or not. It's best to powder golden flax seeds (linseeds) in an electric coffee grinder (or buy them already ground and store them in the refrigerator). Then you can easily sprinkle them over low-carb cereals or mix them into yogurt or protein 'shakes'.

TOFU

A great product, tofu is very high in protein and low in carbs. Make sure it's made from non-GMO (non-genetically modified) soya. I like to use firm tofu (sometimes plain, sometimes smoked) for most recipes but some people prefer to use silken tofu for shakes and sauces, as it has a more liquid, creamy consistency. Cauldron is a very reliable brand of tofu that is widely available.

READY-MADE VEGETARIAN PROTEIN FOODS

The range of protein foods is increasing all the time; some are based on mixtures of soy and wheat protein or from Quorn whereas others are vegetable based. They vary a lot in carb and protein content, so you need to read the labels carefully; some are very low-carb and high in protein whereas others are extremely 'carby' and not a very good source of protein. Also, do buy organic products if you can, because then you know for sure that you will be avoiding genetically modified ingredients. Also, try to avoid foods that contain trans-fats and hydrogenated fat, as these are not healthy fats to include in the diet. (Trans-fats may interfere with the body's omega-3 oils – necessary for brain function, and healthy blood and heart – and, like saturated fats, can raise cholesterol levels.)

TEXTURED VEGETABLE PROTEIN (TVP)

Our old friend from the 1970s, TVP, is dried, extruded soya protein, which is still available from health stores in the form of 'mince' or 'chunks'. It's high in protein, and quite low in carbs. Make sure whichever type you buy is GMO-free.

QUORN

A popular vegetarian ingredient, Quorn is made from micoprotein, which is cultured like yeast. It is rich in protein and quite low in carbs. Although it's not really low enough in carbs for the early stages of low-carb dieting, it can be used to make delicious dishes during Phases 2 and 3. Quorn is not a vegan food because it contains some egg white and sometimes milk products, but many vegetarians are happy to use it now that the manufacturers have guaranteed that the egg white used in Quorn is from free-range eggs. But be careful, this does not apply to all Quorn products, so make sure you buy the ones that have the Vegetarian Society symbol. The carbs in the different products do vary and most of them are rather too high for Phase 1, so check the labels.

PROTEIN POWDERS

Pure microfiltered whey powder and soya protein isolate powder are both useful for boosting protein, particularly when added to smoothies and other drinks. I also use soya protein isolate powder (the protein which has been extracted from soya flour) in some recipes; it has virtually no carbs and a pleasant, neutral flavour. You could substitute soya flour (available from health stores), but this does contain a few carbs and has quite a strong flavour. Both whey powder and soya protein isolate powder are concentrated, so it's important to get good-quality ones. Although they may seem expensive, 'per serving' they probably work out at about half the price of buying a cup of coffee – not bad for around a quarter of your day's protein. Buy the best-quality microfiltered whey powder, and GMO-free soya protein isolate powder.

Gluten powder is another protein powder that is useful in low-carb recipes. Made from the protein part of flour, this is one you cook with rather than using in smoothies and drinks. Gluten powder can be mixed with water and then formed into steaks to make a variety of low-carb foods. It can also be used in baking and for coating burgers and rissoles instead of flour. At the moment it is available only over the internet, although I hope it will soon be stocked by health stores. Find the details of suppliers at Sources and Stockists (see pages 150–1).

SOYA MILK

There is a wide variety of soya milks and they are easily available. Make sure you buy organic (which will not be made with genetically modified soya) and unsweetened. If it says 'plain' on the packet, it may mean it's unflavoured but could still have sugar added, so check. You don't need to buy 'fresh' soya milk from the chill cabinet; the normal, long-life ones are perfectly fine and easier to store.

fats and oils

BUTTER

Buy organic butter to avoid antibiotics, hormones and other chemicals that are often given to animals. Vegans can substitute a pure vegan margarine without trans-fats (available from health stores), but it's best to cook with olive oil rather than this.

CREAM

Organic cream is best, and double cream has fewer carbs than single. Although it may contain a trace of sugar, the soya cream called Soya Dream is very low in carbs; it contains fewer carbs than double cream. Soya Dream is quite widely available from health stores and some large supermarkets in the UK. I love it for everything except adding to hot coffee, when it curdles, or for recipes that require whipped cream, as it won't thicken. You can now buy 'whipping' soya cream, but unfortunately it is sweetened and therefore rather 'carby', and to me it has rather a synthetic taste. Let's hope a non-sweetened version becomes available, as that would be very useful.

COLD-PRESSED VEGETABLE OILS

Choose cold-pressed, organic oils for their health-giving properties as well as flavour. I believe olive oil is the healthiest oil to use for cooking, as well as in dressings. Flax seed oil is an excellent source of omega-3 oils. Buy it from a health store where they store it in the refrigerator; keep it refrigerated when you've bought it, and use it up quickly. Add a teaspoonful to your shakes and salad dressings (never heat it) so that you take about a tablespoonful a day, and you'll never have to worry about supplementing with omega-3 oils again.

COCONUT OIL

You can buy virgin coconut oil, which is actually solid until heated, in a tub at good health and organic shops. It's expensive but goes quite a long way and it keeps well. Although a saturated fat, this has been shown to be a good health-giving oil.

MAYONNAISE

Good-quality bought mayonnaise is virtually carb-free. Check the label – or make your own using the recipe on page 61, which is also suitable for vegans.

sweeteners

Wherever sweetening is called for in a recipe I've suggested 'stevia or your chosen low-carb sweetener'. My first choice is for stevia, a 100-per-cent natural sweetener, which is made from a plant called stevia. However, you can't buy it in the UK (although you can buy it easily over the internet) and not everyone likes the taste. I have left you to decide on your preferred sweetener because many people like to use artificial sweeteners, although, personally, I am not happy about them. In fact I think they may be detrimental to health. So the sweetener you use really does come down to personal choice. As it's an important issue for low-carb cooks, I'm going to repeat here in full what I said about the various sweeteners in *The Vegetarian Low-Carb Diet*, so that you can read the facts and make up your own mind.

Most low-carb diet books, including Atkins, warn against the use of aspartame, which can stall weightloss (and, some people believe, is associated with a host of health problems including migraines and vision problems). Instead, they recommend an artificial sweetener called sucralose. This is marketed under the name Splenda and is available in tablet or granular form. The tablets do not contain any carbs but you have to count 0.5g carbs per teaspoonful for the granular type because the 'bulker' in it is carbohydrate.

SPLENDA

Sucralose, marketed under the name Splenda, is a chlorinated sucrose derivative. There has been no independent, long-term human research on this product. In the view of some leading health experts, the 'hundreds of studies' (some of which show hazards) claimed by the manufacturer were inadequate and do not demonstrate safety in long-term use. Whether you use it or not is, of course, your decision, but I don't use it myself and would not recommend it. For more about this, see Useful Websites under Sources and Stockists (page 151). Splenda is available from any supermarket.

MALTITOL AND XYLITOL

Other low-carb sweeteners include maltitol and xylitol. These are commonly made from corn but, although natural ingredients, they are highly processed. They pass right through the body without being absorbed, so you don't have to count the carbs. However, they do not agree with some people: they can cause digestive upsets, bloating and flatulence. If you can eat them, they may be useful. But go carefully, starting with small quantities. I think these are fine in small amounts if they agree with you, although I don't recommend them for the first fortnight of the Carb Cleanse (see page 6). They are included in many manufactured low-carb products (as is sucralose/Splenda). Read the label and decide for yourself what you do and don't want to put into your body. In my opinion, xylitol is fine for occasional use.

STEVIA

The sweetener I most like to use is stevia. This is about as natural a sweetener as you can get because it is made from a herb. In fact, you can sweeten your tea just by dipping a stevia leaf straight into it. However, it's normally used in the form of a white powder, and that is how I buy it.

Stevia is very, very concentrated: a speck of pure stevia the size of a sesame seed is equivalent to a teaspoonful of sugar. Because it's so concentrated, stevia is often sold mixed with a carbohydrate 'bulker', such as rice powder. You can buy it like this, often in little packets, or you can buy it 'pure' as a more concentrated powder, or in liquid form, in a dropper bottle. There is also a new 'spoonable' type of stevia, which does not contain any carbs and can be obtained over the internet (see Sources and Stockists). I have not had a chance to try this myself yet but have heard good reports about it.

It's worth trying the different types to see which you like. If you use the type with the 'bulker' added, you will have to add on the extra carbs, although they won't increase the total of the recipe a great deal. Personally, I like the pure stevia powder best; I use it in a shaker so that I can add it in tiny quantities, according to taste. (Although I'm looking forward to trying the new spoonable type.)

You can use stevia to sweeten anything, and you can also bake with it, as you will see in the recipe section. Unlike sugar and artificial sweeteners, tests have shown that it is positively good for you. Stevia appears to have a regulating effect on the pancreas. It also helps stabilise blood sugar levels, acts as a general tonic, reduces stomach acid and gas, and inhibits the bacteria that cause dental decay and gum disease.

So, what's the catch? There are two. Firstly, some people don't like the flavour, which is a tiny bit reminiscent of liquorice and ever so slightly bitter (although for me the naturalness of the product outweighs these disadvantages and I've really come to like the flavour). Although pure stevia is about 300 times sweeter than sugar, its sweetness is somehow gentler and subtler than that of sugar and takes a while to get used to.

Secondly, you cannot buy stevia in the UK because it's illegal for anyone to sell it to you. This is because when the European Scientific Commission considered an application for its use, it was presented with what the health writer Leslie Kenton describes as 'rather bogus data'. Based on this data, the Commission concluded that a test-tube derivative of stevia, known as steviol, 'might produce adverse effects in the male reproductive system and damage DNA'. The EU Standing Committee for Foodstuffs decided that the plants and dried leaves of *Stevia rebaudiana* should not be approved 'due to lack of information supporting the safety of the product'. This was difficult to understand, since stevia has been grown, studied and used for centuries in many countries, with no recorded ill effects. It is also used by diabetics in many parts of the world and in about 40 per cent of manufactured sweet products in Japan. One can only conclude that the decision might have had more to do with protecting the sugar and sweetener industries than with concern about people's health and well-being. Unlike sugar and articial sweeteners, I have seen no evidence to suggest that stevia poses any threat to human health.

Stevia can be obtained from the US. There, it has been classified as GRAS (Generally Recognised as Safe) for decades, and used to sweeten tea, amongst other things. Then the FDA (Food and Drug Administration), in a misguided attempt to 'protect' Americans, refused to make it legal. However, after many years of public pressure, it was reclassified as 'Safety Unproven' and it can be found in health stores where it is allowed to be sold as a herb, not as a sweetener. At least you can still buy it there.

Because you need so little, it's light to post, and I find it quite practical to have it sent from the US. I've given details in the Sources and Stockists section of this book (pages 150–1).

Stevia is, in fact, readily available in most countries of the world, including Australia, New Zealand and Canada. According to articles on the Internet, the position is better in these countries and it looks as if there is even a campaign to grow it in Australia, which is fantastic news. Readers in these countries will need to make their own enquiries but I think they may be able to buy it at health stores, perhaps classified as a 'food supplement', as in the US.

fruit and vegetables

Most vegetables and the full range of melons and berries, as well as rhubarb and some other fruits can be used in low-carb cooking, as the recipes in this book demonstrate. As some fruit and vegetables – such as bananas and grapes, potatoes and parsnips – are on the high side, it's best to stick to the low-carb ones until you reach the maintenance stage of the diet.

I personally like to buy organic produce whenever I can, but that doesn't mean it's necessary to stop eating fresh fruit and vegetables if they're not organic. It's still important to use them in the diet; indeed they're one of the mainstays of this diet. Just do your best, and make sure you wash them very well before use.

drinks, shakes and smoothies

GREAT FOR BREAKFAST, light meals or snacks at any time, shakes and smoothies are a particularly pleasant and useful way of boosting your protein and your energy levels, when eating a vegetarian low-carb diet.

Many ingredients can be used: unsweetened soya milk, or a milk made from low-carb nuts or seeds such as almonds makes a particularly good base, or you can use a soya protein isolate powder or microfiltered whey powder with water. Nuts can be added, either finely ground or in the form of nut butter; they enrich and thicken a smoothie or shake, as well as adding flavour. Protein powders or whey powder can be whizzed with water, a strong herb tea, or even coffee, to vary the flavours. Any smoothie can be thickened by adding 55g (2oz) plain tofu (standard or silken) and/or 1–2 tablespoonfuls of finely ground flax seeds or almonds, or 1–3 teaspoons of nut butter – experiment and have fun! The latter also adds flavour and richness but they are very concentrated, so a little goes a long way.

Other flavourings include cocoa powder, which is low in carbs, grated orange or lemon rind, coffee, any spices you fancy – cinnamon, ginger and freshly grated nutmeg work particularly well – also fresh sweet herbs such as mint.

Mint, as well as sage, rosemary and thyme, also makes wonderful teas that are so much fresher and more invigorating than those made from tea bags (see A Nice Pot of Fresh Peppermint Tea, page 28), and spices, especially fresh root ginger and cinnamon, can be used in the same way, and all of these are carb-free!

You will find some recipes and ideas in this section to get you going, but half the fun is experimenting and coming up with your own combinations. You can whisk the mixture, shake it in a lidded flask or blend it using a stick blender, a liquidiser or food processor.

strawberry smoothie

PHASES ❷ ❸

PREPARATION 2–3 MINUTES

100g (3½oz) strawberries
150ml (¼ pint)
   unsweetened soya milk
1 scoop non-GMO soya
   protein isolate powder
55g (2oz) firm tofu
1 tablespoon soya cream
   or double cream
stevia or your chosen low-
   carb sweetener, to taste

Serves 1

This is a fruity smoothie that is also packed with protein. Other low-carb fruits such as raspberries or blackberries can be used instead of strawberries for a change – they all work out at about the same carbs – and you can also freeze the fruits first (or use frozen ones) for a gorgeously thick and creamy shake.

1 Put the strawberries, soya milk, soya protein isolate powder, tofu and cream into a blender, food processor or the goblet that comes with a stick blender, and whizz together for about 15 seconds, until blended.

2 Sweeten to taste with stevia or your choice of low-carb sweetener. Drink immediately.

> **7.3g carbs and 40.5g protein**

melon and mint cooler

PHASES

100g (3½oz) sweet ripe
melon with green or
white flesh (Ogen or
honeydew), weighed
without skin and seeds
2 sprigs of mint
100ml (3½ fl oz) water

Serves 1

PREPARATION 3 MINUTES

Ripe and juicy melon has got to be one of the most thirst-quenching fruits. Frothy and naturally sweet, this smoothie is beautifully refreshing.

1 Put the melon and one of the sprigs of mint into a blender, food processor or the goblet that comes with a stick blender. Add the water and whizz for about 15 seconds, until blended.

2 Pour into a glass, top with the remaining mint sprig. Drink at once.

8.3g carbs and 0.5g protein

lemon cheesecake smoothie

PHASES

PREPARATION 3 MINUTES

finely grated rind of
   1 lemon
1 scoop non-GMO soya
   protein isolate powder
55g (2oz) plain tofu
2 tablespoons soya cream
drop or two of vanilla
   extract
drop or two of lemon
   extract (optional)
150ml (¼ pint) water
stevia or your chosen low-
   carb sweetener, to taste
1 level tablespoon toasted
   flaked almonds, lightly
   crushed

Serves 1

This is actually vegan but tastes so rich, creamy and amazingly like cheesecake that you would never know – and it's very filling and full of nutritious ingredients. It makes a luxurious breakfast, or might just hit that 'cookie' spot in the middle of the morning or afternoon.

1 Reserve a pinch of the grated lemon rind to use for decoration. Put the remainder into a blender, food processor or the goblet that comes with a stick blender. Add the soya isolate powder, tofu, soya cream, vanilla extract and lemon extract, if you're using this. Pour in the water and whizz until blended, thick and creamy, using a little more water if you prefer a thinner consistency.

2 Add stevia or low-carb sweetener to taste. Pour into a glass and top with the crushed almonds and reserved lemon rind. Drink at once.

2.5g carbs and 37g protein

fabulous frapuccino *v*

PHASES

PREPARATION 2–3 MINUTES

1 scoop non-GMO soya
protein isolate powder
55g (2oz) plain tofu
2 tablespoons soya cream
150ml (¼ pint) water
1 teaspoon good-quality
    instant decaffeinated
    coffee
stevia or your chosen low-
    carb sweetener, to taste
    (optional)
sprinkling of cocoa
    powder

Serves 1

This tastes like a thick and creamy frapuccino but is full of protein, so it's a breakfast drink that will take you right through the morning, yet with very few carbs. If that weren't enough, it's also vegan and full of healthy ingredients!

1 Put the soya protein isolate powder into a blender, food processor or the goblet that comes with a stick blender. Add the tofu, soya cream, water and coffee powder, and whizz until thick, creamy and frothy. (Adjust the thickness with a little more water if you wish.)

2 Add stevia or low-carb sweetener to taste. Pour into a glass or mug, sprinkle with a dusting of cocoa powder and drink immediately.

1.7g carbs and 35g protein

iced raspberry shake *V*

PHASES

100g (3½oz) frozen
   raspberries
150ml (¼ pint)
   unsweetened soya milk
1 scoop non-GMO soya
   protein isolate powder
55g (2oz) firm tofu
1 tablespoon soya or
   double cream
stevia or your chosen low-
   carb sweetener, to taste

Serves 1

PREPARATION 5 MINUTES

Using frozen raspberries results in a gorgeously thick and
creamy shake that's also protein-rich and good for you.

1 Put the frozen raspberries into a blender, food processor or
   the goblet that comes with a stick blender. Add the soya
   milk, soya protein isolate powder, tofu and cream, and
   whizz for about 15 seconds, until thick and creamy.

2 Sweeten to taste with stevia or your choice of low-carb
   sweetener. Drink immediately.

7.1g carbs and 41g protein

a nice pot of fresh peppermint tea

PHASES

PREPARATION 5 MINUTES, PLUS 5 MINUTES STANDING TIME

large bunch of mint
boiling water

Makes 4–6 cups

In these tea-bag days, it's easy to forget just how good it is to sit down to a proper pot of tea. This mint tea is wonderful – so fragrant and uplifting, and totally carb-free! If you're within reach of a Middle Eastern shop that's usually the best place to go for lovely large bunches of mint (and other fresh herbs), if you don't grow them yourself.

1 Wash the mint then put it, stalks and all, into a teapot, pushing it down so that the pot is about half-full.

2 Pour in boiling water to fill the pot, then put the lid on and leave to stand for about 5 minutes for the full flavour to develop.

3 Pour into cups. You can top up the pot with more hot water for second cups, and if there's any left over it's also great chilled with some ice and sprigs of mint.

0g carbs and 0g protein per serving

hot and cold breakfasts

BREAKFAST IS A MEAL you really come to appreciate when you are on the vegetarian low-carb diet and experience the steady and sustained energy that a 'good breakfast' can supply. This can be something as simple as a protein shake or smoothie (see previous section), it can be a more conventional muesli-type mixture or cereal, it can be amazing pancakes or waffles, or something hot and savoury. All these options are covered in this section.

I know that a lot of successful vegetarian low-carbers also get into the habit of saving some of their protein from supper the night before to reheat quickly at breakfast time. If this is more vegetable than protein you can always boost it by serving a protein shake alongside. I think the main thing is to plan a little in advance to make it easy for you in the morning and make sure your day gets off to a really 'good breakfast' start.

hot cinnamon cereal **v**

PHASES ① ② ③

PREPARATION 5 MINUTES

2 tablespoons flax seeds
1 tablespoon vanilla-
   flavoured non-GMO
   soya protein isolate
   powder
½ teaspoon ground
   cinnamon or vanilla
   extract
15g (½oz) butter or vegan
   margarine
200ml (7 fl oz) boiling
   water
stevia or artificial
   sweetener to taste
2–3 tablespoons double or
   soya cream
15g (½oz) brazil nuts,
   almonds or walnuts,
   chopped

Serves 1

This is warm and comforting. The ground flax seeds, which are very nutritious (page 15), thicken to a porridge-like consistency and the chopped nuts add some crunch.

1 Grind the flax seeds finely – an electric coffee mill is good for this.

2 Put the ground flax seeds into a bowl with the protein powder and mix well. Then sprinkle with the cinnamon or vanilla and dot with the butter or vegan margarine.

3 Pour the boiling water on top, stirring to avoid lumps. Taste and sweeten as necessary.

4 Swirl the cream over the top, scatter with the chopped nuts and serve immediately.

4.6g carbs and 33.5g protein if using stevia and soya protein isolate powder; for other low-carb sweeteners and protein powders, add on carbs accordingly.

low-carb granola

PREPARATION 10 MINUTES • COOKING 5–7 MINUTES

55g (2oz) unsweetened desiccated coconut

85g (3oz) chopped brazil nuts

85g (3oz) chopped walnuts

85g (3oz) chopped almonds

85g (3oz) sunflower seeds

115g (4oz) melted butter

1 teaspoon ground cinnamon

1 teaspoon vanilla extract

stevia or your chosen low-carb sweetener, to taste

85g (3oz) flax seeds

To serve

plain, Greek or soya yoghurt, soya milk or cream

Makes 8 × 55g (2oz) servings

This is a wonderful golden crunchy granola with a buttery flavour. It's great with yogurt, cream or soya milk.

1 Preheat the oven to 180°C/350°F/Gas 4.

2 Put the coconut, brazil nuts, walnuts, almonds and sunflower seeds onto a baking sheet. Add the melted butter, cinnamon and vanilla extract, stirring gently. Taste a little and add stevia or artificial sweetener to taste.

3 Bake in the oven for about for 5–7 minutes, stirring two to three times until golden brown. Keep an eye on it – granola burns quickly.

4 Remove from the oven and immediately turn into a bowl, to prevent the mixture continuing to cook on the hot baking sheet, and stir in the flax seeds.

5 When it's completely cold, transfer to a storage container. Serve with plain, Greek or soya yogurt, soya milk or cream.

> **34.8g carbs and 84g protein for the whole quantity**
> **4.4g carbs and 10.5g protein per 55g (2oz) serving**

vegan variation
Use coconut oil instead of butter.

ricotta and lemon pancakes

PHASES ① ② ③

PREPARATION 10 MINUTES • **COOKING** 5 MINUTES

4 eggs
1 tablespoon soya flour
4 tablespoons cold water
flavourless cooking oil

For the ricotta filling
250g (9oz) ricotta cheese
180ml (6 fl oz) double
    cream
grated rind of 1 lemon
stevia or your chosen low-
    carb sweetener, to taste

Serves 4

With their creamy, lemony filling and delicate texture these pancakes are exquisite. Serve them as a breakfast treat or special pudding. For a real treat, accompany them with a few raspberries, or some raspberry coulis (page 69).

1 First make the ricotta filling: put the ricotta cheese into a bowl with the cream and lemon rind, and whisk together until thick. Gently stir in stevia or artificial sweetener to taste. Set aside.

2 To make the pancakes, whisk the eggs with the soya flour and water to make a batter.

3 Heat a frying pan and add enough oil to make a thin film. Pour a quarter of the batter into the pan, tilting it to allow the mixture to flow all over the surface. Cook until the pancake is set, then remove it from the pan (no need to flip it over and cook the other side). Transfer to a plate and repeat with the rest of the mixture, to make four pancakes in all.

4 Put a quarter of the ricotta mixture into the centre of a pancake and roll it up. Repeat with the rest, and serve.

5.4g carbs and 14.3g protein per serving

asparagus frittata

PREPARATION 20 MINUTES • **COOKING** 20 MINUTES

250g (9oz) asparagus, trimmed and cut into 5cm (2in) pieces
4 eggs
4 tablespoons freshly grated Pecorino or Parmesan cheese
225g (8oz) spring onions, finely chopped
2 tablespoons olive oil

Serves 2

If you like asparagus, you're in luck with the low-carb diet; it's so low in carbs you can pretty well eat as much as you want. This frittata, in which it is combined with tangy cheese, is a particularly delectable way to enjoy it.

1 Cook the asparagus in boiling water until tender, about 7–10 minutes.

2 Whisk the eggs and add the grated cheese and the spring onions. Preheat the grill.

3 Heat the oil in a large frying pan that can go under the grill. Put in the drained asparagus; stir-fry for a minute, then pour in the beaten eggs, moving the asparagus around gently to make sure the egg mixture gets right through, and that the grated cheese is well distributed.

4 Let the frittata cook over a moderate heat for a few minutes until the underside is cooked and lightly browned. Then pop the frying pan under a hot grill (cover a wooden handle with foil, if necessary) for a minute or two until the top is set and golden brown. Cut the frittata into wedges and serve from the pan.

5.5g carbs and 21.6g protein per serving

orange waffles with blueberries

PHASES

115g (4oz) baking mix, see
    page 144
6 tablespoons butter,
    melted and cooled
4 eggs, beaten
grated rind of 2 oranges
about 250ml (9 fl oz)
    water
oil, for greasing
stevia or granular low-
    carb sugar substitute

To serve
100g (3½oz) blueberries
soured cream (optional)

Serves 4, makes 8
waffles or 12 small
pancakes

PREPARATION 10 MINUTES • **COOKING** ABOUT 5 MINUTES

These are great made with a waffle iron, but if you haven't got one you can still make them in a frying pan, in which case they will come out as little puffy pancakes, like drop scones.

1 Preheat the waffle iron according to the manufacturer's instructions.

2 Put the baking mix into a bowl. Make a well in the centre and stir in the cooled butter, beaten eggs and orange rind. Gradually stir in enough of the water to make a thick batter. You can leave the batter plain, or sweeten it to taste with a little stevia or low-carb sweetener, if you like.

3 Oil the waffle iron. Put about 3 tablespoons of batter into the waffle iron. Close and cook according to the manufacturer's instructions until crisp and golden brown. Repeat with the rest of the batter.

4 Alternatively, heat a little oil in a frying pan (preferably non-stick). Put heaped tablespoons of the batter into the frying pan, leaving room for them to spread a little. When the underside is done and the top set enough to turn, flip them over with a spatula to cook the other side.

5 Serve the waffles or pancakes with blueberries and soured cream if you wish. The blueberries can be very lightly cooked in a pan with a tablespoon of water until the juices run, if you prefer. Add a little stevia or sweetener to taste, if needed.

Dust the waffles with a sprinkling of low-carb sweetener or xylitol before serving, if you like.

> **7.7g carbs and 25.3g protein per serving, for the waffles and blueberries – soured cream is extra**

'potato' pancakes

PHASES

PREPARATION 10 MINUTES • **COOKING** 7–8 MINUTES

225g (8oz) turnips, peeled and coarsely grated
2 spring onions, chopped
1 tablespoon chopped parsley
1 tablespoon non-GMO soya protein isolate powder
1 egg
oil, for shallow frying
salt and freshly ground black pepper

Makes 8

These grated turnip pancakes make very good potato pancake replacements. Serve them with fried mushrooms (for negligible extra carbs), some sliced or fried tomato, which adds on 2–3 carbs, or some salsa.

1 Mix together the grated turnip, chopped spring onion, parsley, soya protein isolate powder and egg. Season with salt and pepper to taste.

2 Heat a thin layer of oil in a frying pan. Add tablespoonfuls of the turnip mixture and press down to make flat pancakes. Fry quite gently so that the inside is cooked, too, until golden brown on one side, then flip them over and fry the other side.

3 Drain on kitchen paper and serve immediately.

> **12.2g carbs and 33.8g protein for the whole quantity**
> **1.5g carbs and 4.2g protein per pancake**

lightly curried eggs

PHASES ① ② ③

4 eggs, hard-boiled
2 tablespoons olive oil
1 small onion, peeled and
   finely chopped
2 teaspoons curry powder
55g (2oz) finely grated
   Cheddar cheese
1 tablespoon milk, soya
   cream or double cream
salt and freshly ground
   black pepper
1–2 tablespoons snipped
   chives, to garnish

Serves 4

PREPARATION 20 MINUTES • **COOKING** 15 MINUTES

If you're tired of scrambled, boiled or fried eggs for breakfast, try these tasty curried eggs for something different – they can be made ahead and kept in the refrigerator until you need them, if you like. They also make a great snack.

1 Remove the shells from the eggs and keep the eggs on one side for the moment.

2 Heat the oil in a medium pan and put in the onions. Fry for 4–5 minutes, or until tender and very lightly browned, then stir in the curry powder and cook for a further minute. Remove from the heat and put half the mixture into a medium bowl.

3 Cut the eggs in half and scoop out the yolks without damaging the whites. Add the yolks to the onion mixture in the bowl, with the grated cheese and the milk or cream. Mix to a thick and soft consistency. Spoon a little of this mixture into the egg whites.

4 Season with salt and pepper, scatter with chives and serve.

2.0g carbs and 10.3g protein per serving

mediterranean tofu scramble

1 small onion, peeled and
   chopped
2 tablespoons olive oil
1 garlic clove, crushed
100g (3½oz) button
   mushrooms, halved
250g (9oz) packet of tofu,
   drained and finely
   crumbled
1 tomato, chopped
2 sun-dried tomatoes,
   chopped
2 tablespoons soy sauce
2 tablespoons chopped
   parsley
2 tablespoons chopped
   basil
salt and freshly ground
   black pepper

Serves 2

PREPARATION 10 MINUTES • **COOKING** 10 MINUTES

Scrambled tofu stands in very well for scrambled eggs in any
vegan kitchen – and makes a tasty change for those who do
eat eggs. I included one version in *The Vegetarian Low-Carb
Diet*; here is a slightly jazzier one with mushrooms, herbs
and tomatoes.

1 In a saucepan fry the onion in the olive oil over a moderate
   heat, for 5–7 minutes, or until tender. Add the garlic and
   mushrooms and cook for 2–3 minutes.

2 Add the tofu to the pan and stir well, then put in the tomato,
   sun-dried tomatoes and soy sauce. Stir well over a gentle
   heat until the tofu is hot and looks like scrambled egg.

3 Remove from the heat, season to taste with salt and pepper,
   stir in the parsley and basil, and serve at once.

9.1g carbs and 23.4g protein per serving

soups

LOW-CARB SOUPS CAN be as warming and satisfying as those that rely on potatoes or flour for thickening – and they can also be indulgently creamy. If potato soup is one of your comfort foods, try the White Vegetable Soup with Paprika, based on cauliflower and flavoured with celery, onion and a touch of thyme, then enriched with cream and swirled with paprika. You could use double cream for this soup, or any of the soups that require cream; it's lower in carbs than single cream and even a little gives a luxurious richness. I also like using soya cream, which is even lower in carbs and, of course, vegan. Just be careful not to let the soup boil after adding it.

I have suggested puréeing these soups to thicken them, although you could leave them chunky or simply purée some of the quantity if you prefer more texture. Unless I'm making a huge quantity I generally use my stick blender directly in the pan to blend the soup, and stop when I get the consistency I want.

Serve the soups as they are, or top them with low-carb garnishes such as croutons made by frying small cubes of low-carb bread, or toasted flaked almonds if you want a crunchy contrast. Or top with grated cheese to turn the soup into a complete meal.

cream of swede soup with cinnamon

PHASES 2 3

PREPARATION 15 MINUTES • **COOKING** 40 MINUTES

15g (½oz) butter
1 tablespoon olive oil
1 onion, peeled and
    chopped
1 cinnamon stick
600g (1lb 5oz) swede
1.5 litres (2¾ pints) water
4 tablespoons soya or
    double cream
salt and freshly ground
    black pepper
chopped fresh parsley,
    to garnish

Serves 4

Although you can make this soup for next to nothing, it tastes surprisingly luxurious with its velvety texture and hint of cinnamon.

1 Melt the butter with the oil in a large saucepan, and add the onion and the cinnamon stick. Cover and cook for 10 minutes. Peel the swede and cut it into small dice, then add these to the pan. Stir, cover and cook gently for a further 5 minutes. Add all of the water and bring to the boil. Simmer for about 20 minutes, or until the swede is very tender.

2 Remove the cinnamon stick, whizz the soup to a smooth purée in a food processor, then pour it through a sieve back into the saucepan. Stir in the cream, and season with salt and freshly ground black pepper. Garnish with chopped parsley.

11g carbs and 2.4g protein per serving

white vegetable soup with paprika

PHASES

PREPARATION 15 MINUTES • **COOKING** 45 MINUTES

1 tablespoon light olive oil
2 celery sticks, chopped
450g (1lb) cauliflower,
   chopped
1 onion, chopped
sprig of fresh thyme
850ml (1½ pints) water
4 tablespoons soya or
   double cream
salt and freshly ground
   black pepper
paprika, to serve

Serves 4

Here is a low-carb version of a comforting potato soup. It looks very pretty garnished with its flush of paprika.

1 Put the oil into a large saucepan and add the celery, cauliflower and onion. Cook, covered, for about 10 minutes, then add the thyme and all of the water. Bring to the boil, turn down the heat and leave the soup to simmer for about 30 minutes, or until the vegetables are very tender.

2 Remove the thyme, liquidise a ladleful of the soup with the cream, then add this to the rest of the soup. Season the soup with salt and pepper, reheat gently, and serve in warmed bowls. Top each with a swirl of paprika.

7.0g carbs and 3.1g protein per serving

stilton soup

PHASES

PREPARATION 10 MINUTES • **COOKING** 1 HOUR 10 MINUTES

350g (12oz) outside celery
  sticks
125g (4½oz) chopped
  onion
850ml (1½ pints) water
1 teaspoon vegetable
  bouillon stock powder
125g (4½oz) Stilton cheese
squeeze of lemon juice
1–2 tablespoons soya or
  double cream
salt and freshly ground
  black pepper
snipped chives or parsley,
  to garnish

Serves 4

Here is a soup recipe that thriftily uses the outer part of a vegetable that you would otherwise throw away. Economical it may be, luxurious it certainly is.

1 Scrub the celery and run a vegetable peeler down each stick to remove (and discard) any stringy bits, then chop and put into a large saucepan with the onion, water and vegetable bouillon powder. Cover, bring to the boil and leave to simmer gently for 1 hour, or until the vegetables are very tender.

2 Put the soup into a food processor and crumble in the cheese in rough chunks. Whizz to a purée, then pour the mixture back into the saucepan through a sieve, pressing through any lumps of cheese.

3 Season with salt and pepper; add a squeeze of fresh lemon juice to sharpen the flavour slightly if necessary, and stir in the cream.

4 Reheat gently, without boiling, then serve in bowls and top each with some chives or parsley.

5.0g carbs and 7.3g protein per serving

cream of celery soup

PREPARATION 15 MINUTES • **COOKING** 1 HOUR 15 MINUTES

2 tablespoons olive oil

2 onions, peeled and
   chopped

450g (1lb) outside sticks of
   celery, trimmed and
   chopped

850ml (1½ pints)
   vegetable stock or water

4 tablespoons soya or
   double cream

salt and freshly ground
   black pepper

a few chopped celery
   leaves, to garnish

Serves 4

This rich and creamy celery soup is perfect for a warming winter lunch. A good vegetable stock will give it a full flavour – home-made is best if you have time but vegetable bouillon is fine if you haven't (vegetable bouillon stock powder is available from health stores).

1 Heat the oil in a large saucepan and add the onions. Cover and cook over a gentle heat for 10 minutes, or until the onions are soft but not browned.

2 Meanwhile, scrub the celery and run a vegetable peeler down each stick to remove any stringy bits. Chop the celery and add it to the onions, stir, cover, and cook for another 5 minutes.

3 Add the stock or water, bring to the boil and leave the soup to cook gently for 1 hour, or until the celery is very tender.

4 Liquidise the soup and pour it through a sieve back into the saucepan to remove any remaining tough pieces of celery. Stir in the cream, and salt and pepper to taste. Serve hot, garnished with the chopped leaves.

6.5g carbs and 1.6g protein per serving

nettle soup *v*

PHASES   ③

1 tablespoon olive oil
1 onion, peeled and
  chopped
450g (1lb) tender nettles
150ml (¼ pint) soya cream
freshly grated nutmeg
1.4 litres (2½ pints) water
salt and freshly ground
  black pepper

Serves 4

PREPARATION 15 MINUTES • **COOKING** 25 MINUTES

Nettles are low in carbs, deliciously health-giving (all that iron!) – and of course free! Pick nettles in the spring and use only the fresh new growth at the top. Choose a non-polluted spot away from car-exhaust fumes. You will need to wear rubber gloves for picking and preparing nettles to avoid being stung.

1 Heat the oil in a large saucepan, put in the onion and cook gently, covered, for 10 minutes.

2 Meanwhile, wash and roughly chop the nettles. Add them to the pan, along with all of the water. Bring to the boil, then simmer for about 15 minutes, or until the nettles are very tender.

3 Whizz to a purée in a food processor and pour back into the pan through a sieve, pushing through as much of the nettles as you can.

4 Stir in the cream, adjust the consistency with a little more water if necessary to make a thin, light soup, then season with freshly grated nutmeg, salt and pepper. Serve in warmed bowls.

4.4g carbs and 4.6g protein per serving

cream of watercress soup

PHASES

PREPARATION 20 MINUTES • **COOKING** 35 MINUTES

1 onion, peeled and diced
1 tablespoon olive oil
75g (2¾oz) turnip, peeled
  and sliced
850ml (1½ pints) water
1 bunch or packet of
  watercress
4 tablespoons double or
  soy cream, plus extra to
  garnish
freshly grated nutmeg
salt and freshly ground
  black pepper

Serves 4

Peppery watercress makes a superb low-carb soup when thickened with turnip. It's full of flavour and deliciously creamy. I like to use the watercress raw in this soup because it makes the flavour of the soup so fresh as well as preserving more of the vitamins.

1 Fry the onion in the oil in a large covered saucepan for 5 minutes, or until the onion becomes soft but not browned. Add the turnip and cook, covered, for a further 5 minutes.

2 Add all of the water, bring to the boil and simmer for about 20 minutes, or until the turnip is tender.

3 Liquidise the soup thoroughly with the watercress, then pour it back into the saucepan and stir in the cream, and nutmeg, salt and pepper to taste. To serve, garnish with the cream.

3.8g carbs and 0.9g protein per serving

salads

HAVING A MAIN-COURSE salad lunch is definitely a satisfying way to avoid the ubiquitous sandwich, and a lot more interesting, too. Such a lunch can be incredibly simple, such as nuts, cheese, hardboiled eggs or a cold, bought low-carb vegetarian protein food such as sausages and all the leafy green vegetables, radishes, celery or kohlrabi sticks that you want. Or it can be an elaborate feast for high days and holidays. The salads in this section cover all events.

There is the stunningly simple Japanese-Style Salad or try Kohlrabi and Radish Salad, which couldn't be easier to make, yet both are interesting as well as refreshing. For a neat low-carb sandwich replacement, try the Lettuce Salad Wraps. There are plenty of simple leafy mixtures including Bitterleaf Salad with Walnut Dressing, and Watercress and Red Pepper with Mascarpone, with its striking colours and contrasts of texture between crisp vegetables and smooth, creamy cheese. Even salads for chilly days are catered for: enjoy the comforting Warm Red Cabbage and Cherry Tomato Salad. If you want something a little more rich, try the gorgeous Baby Vegetables with Aioli, and, if you feel like making an effort for that special occasion, the Salad Roulade makes a dramatic centrepiece and everyone loves it.

bitterleaf salad
with walnut dressing

PHASES

PREPARATION 10 MINUTES

2 chicory

1 radicchio

1 oak leaf lettuce

2 tablespoons snipped
chives

55g (2oz) chopped walnuts

For the dressing

2 tablespoons olive oil

1 tablespoon walnut oil

1 tablespoon red wine
vinegar

salt and freshly ground
black pepper

Serves 4

The 'bitter leaves' – chicory and radicchio – make a refreshing salad that contrasts particularly well with cheese dishes. The addition of the walnuts is classically French and gives texture as well as flavour.

1 Separate all the leaves, and then wash and dry them.

2 Make a dressing straight into the bowl by mixing together the oils, vinegar, and salt and pepper.

3 Tear the leaves into the bowl and add the snipped chives. Just before you want to serve the salad, toss the leaves so that they are all coated in the dressing, and then add the walnuts.

5.4g carbs and 4.7g protein per serving

lettuce salad wraps

PHASES

125g (4½oz) full-fat,
   low-carb cream cheese
55g (2oz) finely grated
   Cheddar cheese
2–3 teaspoons
   mayonnaise
3–4 large lettuce leaves
   (iceberg is ideal)
½ tomato, thinly sliced

Serves 1

PREPARATION 10 MINUTES

These are a neat replacement for sandwiches and you can use all kinds of different fillings – chopped hardboiled eggs, any cheese (as long as it's low-carb), marinated tofu, a little peanut butter mixed with chopped celery, fingers of feta cheese with chopped herbs and olives, in fact any low-carb protein mixture you fancy.

1 Mix together the cream cheese, finely grated Cheddar and enough mayonnaise to bind the mixture.

2 Spoon some of the cheese mixture onto a lettuce leaf, top with a thin slice of tomato and roll the leaf around the filling to make a neat package like a stuffed vine leaf. Repeat with the rest of the filling and leaves.

> **6.8g carbs and 24g protein per serving**

vegan variation
Use vegan cream cheese and finely grated vegan hard cheese and mayonnaise. Read the packets for carb and protein information, as these vary.

piquant cucumber salad

PHASES

PREPARATION 10 MINUTES, PLUS AT LEAST 1 HOUR STANDING

1 cucumber
2 teaspoons white
   mustard seeds
3 tablespoons rice vinegar
   or white wine vinegar
salt and freshly ground
   black pepper
fresh chives or young dill,
   to garnish

Serves 4

Mustard seeds give this refreshing cucumber salad a pleasant kick. It makes an unusual and cooling starter.

1 Peel the cucumber then cut it into fairly thin slices. Layer these into a shallow dish, sprinkling the mustard seeds, some salt and a grinding of pepper between the layers. Pour the vinegar over the top.

2 Cover the salad and leave for at least 1 hour, preferably longer – or even overnight – for the flavours to blend. Sprinkle over some snipped fresh chives or dill before serving.

2.7g carbs and 0.9g protein per serving

chicory, red leaf and watercress salad

PHASES   ❸   PREPARATION 15 MINUTES

2 heads of chicory

1 red lettuce such as feuille
   de chêne (oakleaf) or
   frisée

1 bunch or packet of
   watercress

1 tablespoon red wine
   vinegar

3 tablespoons olive oil

salt and freshly ground
   black pepper

Serves 4

Serve this pretty and refreshing salad for lunch with a tasty main course such as Tarragon, Almond and Pecorino Tart, and I guarantee no one will know you are on a diet, especially if you finish the meal with a luxurious pudding like raspberries and cream. That's one of the joys of low-carb dieting, including, of course, the way the pounds come off!

1 Wash and dry the chicory, red lettuce and watercress.

2 Put the red wine vinegar into a large bowl with the olive oil, some salt and a good grinding of pepper.

3 Tear the chicory and frisée into manageable pieces and put them into the bowl on top of the dressing. Add the watercress.

4 Toss the salad just before you are ready to serve it.

1.4g carbs and 1.3g protein per serving

salad roulade

PHASES

PREPARATION 45 MINUTES • **COOKING** 15 MINUTES

butter, for greasing
ready-grated Parmesan
   cheese, for coating
55g (2oz) cream cheese
4 eggs, separated
150ml (¼ pint) soya cream
200g (7oz) Gruyère
   cheese, grated
salt and freshly ground
   black pepper

For the filling
2 heaped tablespoons
   mayonnaise
3 flexible lettuce leaves
2 tomatoes, skinned
2 spring onions, finely
   chopped

Serves 4

This might seem a bit fiddly to make, but with minimum carbs and maximum impact it's worth it for a special lunch or first course. I use soya cream for its lower carbs and unsaturated fat, but you could use whipping cream with slightly higher carbs (1g more per serving).

1 Preheat the oven to 200°C/400°F/Gas 6. Line a 33 × 23cm (13 × 9in) Swiss roll tin with a piece of baking parchment – it needn't be too tidy. Grease the paper and sprinkle with the grated Parmesan cheese.

2 Put the cream cheese and egg yolks into a large bowl and mix together until smooth. Gradually mix in the cream and then stir in the grated Gruyère cheese. In another bowl, whisk the egg whites until stiff, then fold them into the Gruyère mixture. Season as necessary with salt and pepper.

3 Pour the mixture into the lined tin, smoothing it gently to the edges and making sure it's even. Bake for 12–15 minutes, or until risen and just firm in the centre. Remove from the oven.

4 Have ready a piece of baking parchment spread out on the work surface and sprinkled with ready-grated Parmesan cheese. Turn the roulade straight out, face down, onto the baking parchment. Cover with a clean, slightly damp tea towel and leave to cool. (It needs to be cool enough not to wilt the salad filling.)

5 Spread the cooled roulade with the mayonnaise, then put the lettuce leaves on top. Slice the tomatoes very thinly and put these on top of the lettuce. Finally, scatter over the spring onions and some salt and pepper.

6 Roll up the roulade, starting from one of the long edges. (It's easiest to do this if you first make an incision about 1cm (½in) from the edge, but don't cut right through, then bend this down to start the rolling process.) Use the paper to help you to roll it firmly. Transfer the roulade to a long serving dish to serve.

3.9g carbs and 26.9g protein per serving

green salad with toasted hazelnuts

PHASES

2–4 chargrilled baby
   artichoke hearts, sliced
   or 1 avocado, peeled
   and sliced
red-leaf lettuce
1 bunch or packet of
   watercress
1 celery heart
2 tablespoons snipped
   fresh chives
55g (2oz) toasted
   hazelnuts, chopped

For the dressing
1 tablespoon hazelnut oil
   (optional)
2 tablespoons olive oil (or
   3 tablespoons if you are
   not using hazelnut oil)
1 tablespoon wine vinegar
salt and freshly ground
   black pepper

Serves 4

PREPARATION 15 MINUTES

Hazelnuts are good value carb-wise and give this salad a nice crunch. You could also vary it by using walnuts and walnut oil for a change. Artichoke hearts are a delicious treat, and quite low in carbs.

1 Mix the dressing ingredients in a salad bowl: put in the hazelnut oil, if using, the olive oil, wine vinegar and some salt and freshly ground black pepper, and mix together well.

2 Add the artichoke hearts or avocado, and mix gently.

3 Wash the lettuce and watercress. Shake dry, and put them into the bowl, tearing large pieces as necessary. Slice the celery heart finely, and add that to the bowl with the chives.

4 Just before you want to serve the salad, turn it gently so that all the leaves get lightly coated with the dressing, and add the chopped nuts.

4g carbs and 4.8g protein per serving

warm red cabbage and cherry tomato salad

PHASES ② ③

450g (1lb) red cabbage

1 onion

2 tablespoons olive oil

2 tablespoons red wine vinegar

225g (8oz) cherry tomatoes, halved

4 tablespoons snipped chives

salt and freshly ground black pepper

Serves 4

PREPARATION 15 MINUTES • **COOKING** 10–15 MINUTES

Halfway between a cooked dish and a salad, this is lovely on a chilly day. Add cubes of feta cheese, hard-boiled eggs or marinated tofu to make a complete main course.

1 Wash and shred the cabbage as finely as you can. Peel and thinly slice the onion.

2 Heat the oil in a large saucepan and put in the cabbage and onion. Cover and cook gently for about 10 minutes, or until the cabbage is tender, stirring from time to time. Finally, add the vinegar. This stage can be done in advance, if you like.

3 Just before you want to serve the salad, gently reheat the cabbage. Stir in the cherry tomatoes and chives. Check the seasoning and serve.

9.7g carbs and 2.5g protein per serving

watercress and red pepper
with mascarpone

PHASES

PREPARATION 5 MINUTES • **COOKING** 20 MINUTES

2 large red peppers
1 bunch or packet of
   watercress
6 tablespoons olive oil
2 tablespoons wine
   vinegar
225g (8oz) mascarpone
salt and freshly ground
   black pepper

Serves 4

This is equally nice as a light meal or starter. If you prepare the pepper in advance, have the watercress washed and the dressing already made in a jar, the dish can be assembled in moments. Incidentally, I don't always bother to skin the peppers after grilling so, as far as I'm concerned, this process is optional.

1 Quarter the red peppers, then put them shiny-side up on a grill pan, and grill at full heat until the skin has blistered and begun to char. Move them halfway through the grilling so that all the skin is cooked. Leave until they're cool enough to handle, then slip off the skins with a sharp knife – they will come off easily – and rinse the peppers under running water to remove the seeds. Cut the peppers into long, thin strips. Put them into a shallow container, cover and keep cool.

2 Wash and remove the stems from the watercress as necessary; put into a polythene bag in the bottom of the refrigerator until required. Make a quick vinaigrette by pouring the oil into a jar with the vinegar, some salt and a grinding of pepper. Shake well, then keep until required.

3 To serve, put some sprigs of watercress on four small plates and arrange some red pepper on top, dividing it among the plates. Then, using two teaspoons, put heaped teaspoons of mascarpone dotted around on top, about five to a plate.

Coarsely grind some black pepper over the mascarpone. Give the vinaigrette a quick shake, then spoon a little over each plate.

4.9g carbs and 2.0g protein per serving

fennel, tomato and black olive salad   *v*

PHASES

PREPARATION 10 MINUTES

2 fennel bulbs, tough parts
   removed, sliced
4 tomatoes, sliced
a handful of black olives

For the dressing
3 tablespoons olive oil
1 tablespoon red wine
   vinegar
salt and freshly ground
   black pepper

Serves 4

The crisp texture and aniseed flavour of fennel is fabulous in a salad and goes particularly well with tomatoes and olives. It makes a good partner for cheese dishes.

1. Make the dressing straight into a salad bowl by mixing together the oil, vinegar and salt and pepper to taste.

2. Put the fennel, tomatoes and black olives into the bowl and toss gently. Serve.

8.6g carbs and 2.7g protein per serving

baby vegetables with aioli

PREPARATION 30 MINUTES • **COOKING** 8 MINUTES

4 baby fennel, halved

4 baby turnips

1 small cauliflower or 2–4 miniature ones, halved or quartered as necessary

225g (8oz) baby courgettes

4 very small baby carrots, about 75g (2¾oz) in total

For the aioli

2–3 garlic cloves

1 egg

¼ teaspoon salt

¼ teaspoon mustard powder

2 or 3 grindings of black pepper

2 teaspoons wine vinegar

2 teaspoons lemon juice

200ml (7 fl oz) light olive oil or grapeseed oil

Serves 4

Warm baby vegetables with garlic mayonnaise – aioli – make a wonderfully indulgent yet (carbwise) guilt-free starter for a treat. You do need a blender or food processor for this quick version of aioli. It's important for the vegetables to be roughly similar in size so that they cook in the same amount of time, so cut them if necessary, or cook the slower ones for a minute or two before adding the others.

1 To make the aioli, put the garlic in a food processor or blender and purée it as smoothly as you can. Add the egg, salt, mustard, pepper, vinegar and lemon juice. Blend for 1 minute at medium speed until the ingredients are well mixed, then turn the speed up to high and gradually add the oil, drop by drop, through the top of the goblet. When you have added about half the oil, you will hear the sound change to a 'glug-glug' noise and you can then add the remainder of the oil more quickly, in a thin stream. Taste the aioli and adjust the seasoning if necessary. If it seems a bit on the thick side, you can thin it by beating in a teaspoon or two of boiling water.

2 Cook the vegetables for about 8 minutes in boiling water, or until just tender. Drain and rinse under the cold tap to cool quickly, then put them into a colander to drain thoroughly.

3 Put the aioli into a shallow bowl on a large platter. Arrange the vegetables around it, patting them dry on kitchen paper as necessary before serving.

8.9g carbs and 4.7g protein per serving

vegan variation **V**

A garlicky version of the Eggless Mayo, page 61, can be used instead of the aioli given here, for a very good vegan version.

kohlrabi and radish salad **V**

PHASES

PREPARATION 10 MINUTES

3 tablespoons olive oil
1 tablespoon wine vinegar
2 kohlrabi or turnip, about 225g (8oz) in total
1 bunch or packet of radishes
salt and freshly ground black pepper

Serves 4

Radishes and kohlrabi have a similar crunchy texture but their flavours are different, making them ideal partners in this simple salad.

1 Put the oil and vinegar into a bowl with salt and pepper to taste and mix to make a simple dressing.

2 Peel the kohlrabi quite thinly, then cut it into julienne matchsticks. Wash, trim and slice the radishes.

3 Add the kohlrabi and radishes to the bowl and stir gently to coat everything with the dressing. Serve.

2.1g carbs and 1.2g protein per serving using kohlrabi
3.3g carbs and 0.75g protein per serving using turnip

Japanese-style salad with dipping sauce and gomasio

PHASES 3

PREPARATION 10 MINUTES • COOKING 2 MINUTES

1 bunch or packet of
   radishes
1 bunch of spring onions
225g (8oz) mooli (see page
   75) or turnip

For the dip
1 tablespoon grated fresh
   root ginger
2 tablespoons soy sauce
2 tablespoons rice vinegar

For the gomasio
4 tablespoons sesame
   seeds
1 teaspoon salt

Serves 4

This is a light and refreshing first course. If you can't get
rice vinegar, ordinary wine vinegar will do, but only use
1 tablespoonful, as it has a stronger flavour. Gomasio is a
seasoning mixture made of ground sesame seeds and salt,
used especially in Japanese cooking.

1 Wash and trim the radishes and spring onions. Peel the mooli
   or turnip and cut into matchsticks. Arrange all the vegetables
   on a serving plate.

2 Make the dip by mixing together all the ingredients and then
   transferring it to a serving bowl.

3 Make the gomasio by putting the sesame seeds and salt into
   a dry frying pan set over a moderate heat. Stir for a couple of
   minutes or so, until the sesame seeds toast and smell nutty
   and delicious, then remove from the heat. Pulverise the seeds
   in a coffee grinder or using a pestle and mortar, and transfer
   to a bowl to serve.

6g carbs and 3.2g protein per serving

sauces, salsas and dressings

YOU DON'T NEED CARBY ingredients, such as flour or sugar, to make some delicious sauces and dressings, as the recipes in this section show. The Quick Creamy Cheese Sauce, for example, really lives up to its name and, in fact, it reminds me of the kind of traditional cheese sauce that my mother used to make. It turns cooked low-carb vegetables into a main course. If you don't like cheese, or are a vegan, there are several other fabulous sauces: the Creamy Tomato Sauce and the Fresh Tomato Sauce as well as the light and naturally sweet Red Pepper Sauce and the robust Rich Mushroom Gravy and Porcini Sauce – each one is different but they all have that special something. And, if you're looking for a fresh, quick and fat-free accompaniment to a dish, the Celery and Tomato Salsa, spiced with chilli and coriander, is hard to beat.

Making a dressing doesn't pose many problems for the low-carb cook because olive oil can be used freely; buy the best extra virgin olive oil that you can and enjoy it in lovely vinaigrettes. I have also included in this chapter an Eggless Mayo – but for that one you need a good-quality oil with a very light flavour, such as one labelled 'mild, light', or grapeseed oil. I developed this recipe because I wanted to make a truly good mayonnaise without egg yolks, for reasons of animal welfare as well as food safety, and I think this recipe lives up to its name. See what you think.

quick creamy cheese sauce

PHASES

15g (½oz) butter
2 tablespoons double
   cream
55g (2oz) cream cheese
55g (2oz) grated Cheddar
   cheese
pinch of mustard powder
   or cayenne pepper
salt and freshly ground
   black pepper

Serves 1, makes 100ml
(3½ fl oz)

PREPARATION 10 MINUTES • **COOKING** 5 MINUTES

This is rich and creamy and quick to whizz up. Pour it over any cooked low-carb vegetables, such as cauliflower, broccoli, mushrooms, asparagus or courgettes, for a satisfying meal in moments.

1 Melt the butter in a saucepan then add the cream, the cream cheese, grated Cheddar cheese and mustard or cayenne pepper. Stir over a gentle heat for a few minutes, or until the ingredients have melted into a creamy sauce.

2 Remove from the heat and add seasoning to taste – a grinding of pepper, but salt may not be needed.

3 Serve at once.

3.2g carbs and 19g protein per serving

eggless mayo ⓥ

3 tablespoons soya milk
¼–½ teaspoon salt
½ teaspoon mustard
  powder
300ml (½ pint) oil
1 dessertspoonful white
  wine vinegar
touch of stevia or your
  chosen low-carb
  sweetener, to taste
salt and freshly ground
  black pepper

Makes 200ml (7 fl oz)

PREPARATION 10 MINUTES

This is a wonderful, thick, luxurious-tasting mayonnaise that's completely egg-free – and I think it's better than Hellmann's! It's easy to make and keeps well in the refrigerator. For best results, use a delicate, light olive oil (look for those labelled 'mild, light'), or a good-quality flavourless oil such as grapeseed. You could use red wine vinegar for this; it turns the mixture very slightly pink but tastes fine. Serve with crunchy salads or to liven up hardboiled eggs.

1 Put the soya milk into a bowl, food processor, blender or the goblet that comes with a stick blender, and mix with the salt and mustard powder.

2 Gradually beat in the oil, drop by drop – through the top of the machine if you're using a food processor or blender, whisking all the time if doing it by hand – until the mixture starts to thicken. Once this happens, you can add the oil in larger amounts, until it's all in, and the mixture is thick and creamy.

3 Stir in the vinegar, taste and add seasoning. Perhaps add a tiny touch of stevia or sweetener to taste, if needed.

virtually carb-free, 1.8g protein

tomato and red wine sauce

PHASES

PREPARATION 15 MINUTES • COOKING 20 MINUTES

1 small onion, peeled and
   sliced
1 celery stick, chopped
1 garlic clove, crushed
1 tablespoon olive oil
sprig of fresh thyme
1 glass (75ml/2½ fl oz) red
   wine
1 × 400g (14oz) can
   tomatoes
salt and freshly ground
   black pepper

Makes 300ml (½ pint)

Red wine gives this tomato sauce a good, rich flavour. Use to brighten up vegetable dishes and to make egg and nut dishes extra tasty.

1 Fry the onion, celery and garlic in the olive oil with the thyme for 10 minutes, browning them slightly. Add the wine and tomatoes. Bring to the boil, then let the sauce bubble away for about 5 minutes, to cook the tomatoes and thicken a bit.

2 Liquidise the sauce, then pour it through a sieve into a saucepan and reheat. Season with salt and pepper.

> **23.5g carbs and 9.4g protein for the whole quantity**
> **1.2g carbs and 0.5g protein per tablespoonful**

celery and tomato salsa

PHASES ❶ ❷ ❸

PREPARATION 10 MINUTES

225g (8oz) tomatoes

1 celery heart

2 tablespoons freshly
   squeezed lemon juice

4 tablespoons chopped
   fresh coriander

chilli powder, to taste

salt and freshly ground
   black pepper

Serves 4

Fresh coriander is the magic ingredient that makes a salsa particularly fine. Here, it makes full-flavoured tomatoes and celery hearts into a refreshing accompaniment to all kinds of dishes, especially Courgettes Parmesan (see page 110) and other baked cheese dishes, and it is so quick to make.

1 Chop the tomatoes coarsely, discarding any tough parts of stem. Slice the celery heart.

2 Put the tomatoes and celery into a bowl with the lemon juice, chopped coriander, and the chilli powder, salt and pepper to taste. Serve immediately.

3g carbs and 1.8g protein per serving

red pepper sauce

PHASES

2 tablespoons olive oil
2 onions, peeled and sliced
2 red peppers, deseeded
   and roughly chopped
150ml (¼ pint) stock
salt and freshly ground
   black pepper

Serves 4

PREPARATION 10 MINUTES • **COOKING** 20 MINUTES

Sauces make so much difference to a meal and this luscious red pepper sauce will look stunning as well as tasting great. Excellent served with many dishes, especially Grilled Courgette with Halloumi Cheese (page 85) and Deep-fried Camembert (page 91).

1 Heat the oil in a saucepan, add the onions and cook, covered, for 5 minutes.

2 Add the peppers to the onions, cover the pan again and cook gently for a further 5 minutes.

3 Pour in the stock, cover and simmer for about 10 minutes, or until the peppers are tender.

4 Liquidise the sauce, strain it into a saucepan, reheat and season to taste.

> **32.9g carbs and 6.3g protein for the whole quantity**
> **8.2g carbs and 1.6g protein per serving**

rich mushroom gravy

PHASES 2 3

PREPARATION 10 MINUTES • **COOKING** 15–20 MINUTES

2 tablespoons olive oil
1 small onion, peeled and
   chopped
1 garlic clove, crushed
175g (6oz) mushrooms,
   chopped
600ml (1 pint) water
2 teaspoons cornflour
2–4 tablespoons soy sauce
1 teaspoon vegetarian
   bouillon stock powder
1 teaspoon yeast extract
salt and freshly ground
   black pepper

Serves 6

Serve this lovely full-flavoured gravy with low-carb veggie sausages and creamy cauliflower mash!

1 Heat the oil in a medium saucepan, put in the onion and cook it, uncovered, for 5 minutes, so that it browns a little. Add the garlic, some ground black pepper and the mushrooms, and cook for a further 5 minutes, continuing the browning process.

2 Add all of the water and bring to the boil. Blend the cornflour with some of the soy sauce, add some of the boiling liquid, then tip the whole lot back into the pan.

3 Stir in the bouillon powder and yeast extract, then let the mixture simmer gently for about 10 minutes, to thicken and give the flavours a chance to develop. Adjust the seasoning as necessary – you may not need any salt.

> **20.5g carbs and 12g protein for the whole quantity**
> **3.4g carbs and 2g protein per serving**

porcini sauce Ⓥ

PHASES ① ② ③

20g (¾oz) dried porcini
    mushrooms
850ml (1½ pints)
    vegetable stock
55g (2oz) butter or vegan
    margarine
1 tablespoon Madeira or
    brandy
1 tablespoon double or
    soya cream
salt and freshly ground
    black pepper

Serves 4

PREPARATION 10 MINUTES, PLUS AT LEAST 1 HOUR STEEPING
COOKING 20 MINUTES

Because of their strong and savoury flavour just a few porcini mushrooms will make a rich and tasty sauce that is perfect for a special meal. Serve it with the Ricotta Rissoles (page 87), or to turn it into a special feast, the Divine Cauliflower Bake (page 117) .

1 Soak the porcini mushrooms in water for 3 minutes, then rinse thoroughly to get rid of any grit. Put them into a saucepan with the stock and bring to the boil. Remove from the heat and leave them to soak for at least 1 hour, or even overnight. After this, strain the stock into a bowl and chop the porcini finely.

2 Melt the butter or vegan margarine in a medium saucepan and add the porcini. Cook over a gentle heat for 5 minutes, then add the liquid you drained off the porcini. Bring to the boil, and let the mixture bubble away for several minutes, or until it is reduced by half.

3 Stir in the Madeira or brandy and the cream, and season with salt and freshly ground black pepper.

1.0g carbs and 0.6g protein per serving

creamy tomato sauce

PHASES

1 tablespoon olive oil
1 small onion, peeled and
   finely chopped
450g (1lb) tomatoes
2 tablespoons double or
   soya cream
salt and freshly ground
   black pepper

Serves 4

PREPARATION 15 MINUTES • **COOKING** 20 MINUTES

When tomatoes are in season and you can buy lovely ripe ones cheaply, try this sauce, which really makes the most of them. If you can't get good fresh tomatoes, it's better to use canned ones instead – two 425g (15oz) cans would be right for this recipe. This rich sauce adds colour as well as flavour to jazz up simple vegetable dishes.

1 Heat the oil in a large saucepan and add the onion. Fry for 5 minutes without browning.

2 Meanwhile, quarter the tomatoes and add them to the pan. Cover and cook over a gentle heat for 10–15 minutes, or until the tomatoes have collapsed. Liquidise the sauce, sieve and then season with salt and pepper.

3 Just before you want to serve the sauce, reheat it gently and add the cream. Check the seasoning, then serve.

4.3g carbs and 1.3g protein per serving

vinaigrette Ⓥ

PHASES ❶ ❷ ❸

2 tablespoons red wine
  vinegar
6 tablespoons olive oil
1–3 teaspoons Dijon
  mustard
salt and freshly ground
  black pepper

Makes 125ml (¼ pint)

PREPARATION 5 MINUTES

For a virtually carb-free dressing for salad that tastes
delicious, you really can't beat a home-made vinaigrette.
Make it straight into a jar and keep it handy for instant use.
It keeps for about 4–6 weeks in the refrigerator, so you can
multiply the quantities, if you like.

Put the vinegar and oil into a screw-top jar with the mustard
and a good seasoning of salt and pepper. Shake well until they
emulsify. Crushed garlic or chopped fresh herbs are nice
additions to this basic vinaigrette.

virtually carb-free, 0g protein

raspberry coulis

PHASES

PREPARATION 5 MINUTES

350g (12oz) fresh or frozen raspberries, thawed
water as required
stevia or your chosen low-carb sweetener, to taste

Serves 4

You can use raspberries to make a thin coulis, or use less water and make a thicker version, which makes a good jam-replacement. Serve the coulis with melon or peaches, or with Greek yogurt.

1 Blend the raspberries in a food processor or blender until puréed.

2 To make a coulis, add about 2 tablespoons water and then pass the mixture through a sieve to make it smooth. To make a jam-like consistency you probably won't need any water nor will you need to sieve it unless you want a smooth 'jam'.

3 Stir in stevia or sweetener to taste. Keep in the refrigerator until needed – it will keep for about 2–3 days.

4.5g carbs and 0.9g protein per serving
0.8g carbs and negligible protein per tablespoon

dips and dippers

THE DIPS IN THIS section make great snacks, nibbles or starters, or they can be part of a packed or salad lunch. They have varying amounts of protein – and of carbs, for that matter – so you'll need to plan the rest of the dishes around them accordingly if you are making a meal of them.

One way of introducing protein for very few carbs is to serve the dip with a protein-rich dipper. Both the Tofu Crisps and the Cheese Crackers are tasty possibilities – and the Courgette Chips are fun to try if you want something hot for dipping. Crisp raw vegetables can also be very low in carbs and are great with the cheese dips or if you are not looking for extra protein.

mushroom 'caviar'

PHASES ❷ ❸

15g (½oz) dried porcini
mushrooms
450g (1lb) mushrooms
1 garlic clove, peeled
2–4 tablespoons chopped
fresh parsley
25g (1oz) butter or vegan
margarine
squeeze of fresh lemon
juice
salt and freshly ground
black pepper

To serve
a little soured cream
(optional)
paprika
sprigs of flat-leaf parsley

Serves 4

PREPARATION 20 MINUTES, PLUS 1 HOUR SOAKING
COOKING 20 MINUTES

Mushroom 'caviar' can be served on celery sticks, pieces of
cucumber or thin slices of raw cauliflower. The dried porcini
mushrooms in the mixture give it lots of extra flavour.

1 Soak the porcini mushrooms in water for 3 minutes, then
rinse thoroughly to get rid of any grit. Put them in a bowl
with boiling water to cover, and leave to soak for 1 hour. Drain
and reserve the liquid.

2 Put the soaked mushrooms and their liquid in a food processor
with the ordinary mushrooms, the garlic and the parsley.
Whizz until everything is finely chopped. Alternatively, chop all
these ingredients by hand; get them as fine as you can.

3 Heat the butter or vegan margarine in a large saucepan and
put in the chopped ingredients. Stir, then cook uncovered for
15–20 minutes, or until all liquid has boiled away.

4 Remove the pan from the heat and season with salt, pepper
and a squeeze of lemon juice. Serve in a bowl. It can also be
served hot, warm or cold on individual plates, with a heaped
teaspoonful of soured cream, a sprinkling of paprika and a
sprig of flat-leaf parsley on each.

13.5g carbs and 16g protein for the whole quantity
3.4g carbs and 4g protein per serving

wild mushroom dip

PHASES **1** **2** **3**

10g (¼oz) dried porcini
    mushrooms
125g (4½oz) wild
    mushrooms
25g (1oz) butter
225g (8oz) cream cheese
salt and freshly ground
    black pepper

Serves 4

PREPARATION 10 MINUTES, PLUS 1 HOUR SOAKING
COOKING 15 MINUTES

If you've just got a few precious wild mushrooms, this dip makes the most of them, and the addition of some porcini intensifies the flavour. A low-carb luxury dish!

1 Soak the porcini mushrooms in water for 3 minutes, then rinse thoroughly to get rid of any grit. Put them in a bowl with boiling water to cover, and leave to soak for 1 hour. Strain and reserve the liquid.

2 Quickly rinse the wild mushrooms and pat dry with kitchen paper. Chop them with the soaked porcini and cook them in the butter for 5 minutes.

3 Add the reserved soaking liquid and cook for a further 10 minutes, or until nearly all the liquid has gone and the mushrooms are tender. Cool.

4 Mix the mushrooms with the cream cheese and season with salt and freshly ground black pepper.

2.2g carbs and 5.2g protein per serving

vegan variation **V**
Use vegan cream cheese (check the carbs) and vegan margarine.

goat's cheese dip

PHASES

100g (3½oz) soft goat's
  cheese
100g (3½oz) Greek yogurt
a little milk or soured
  cream
freshly ground black
  pepper

Serves 4

This cheese dip is great for a nibble with crudités or with salad for a light meal (in which case it would serve two people).

1 Mix the goat's cheese and Greek yogurt in a food processor until creamy.

2 Add a little milk or soured cream to soften it, and season with pepper.

1.5g carbs and 6.9g protein per serving

fresh herb dip

PHASES ❶ ❷ ❸

PREPARATION 5 MINUTES

300ml (½ pint) crème
  fraîche
3–4 tablespoons chopped
  fresh herbs, such as
  chives, marjoram and
  chervil, as available
salt and freshly ground
  black pepper

Serves 4

You can create a variety of flavours for this refreshing, creamy dip depending on the fresh herbs available. Tasty any time, but also ideal for a party.

Put the crème fraîche into a bowl then stir in the chopped fresh herbs and some salt and freshly ground black pepper to taste.

2g carbs and 1.4g protein per serving

blue cheese dip

PHASES ❶ ❷ ❸

PREPARATION 5 MINUTES

100g (3½oz) blue cheese
100g (3½oz) cream cheese
freshly ground pepper
salt, if needed

Serves 4

Like the Goat's Cheese Dip, this is also good with salad as a light meal, when this quantity would serve two people – so simple but so tasty.

Either whizz the blue cheese and cream cheese in a food processor, or crumble the blue cheese into a bowl then mash with a fork, gradually adding the cream cheese until the mixture is smooth and creamy. Season with pepper and a little salt, if necessary.

1.25g carbs and 7.25g protein per serving

daikon 'crisps'

PHASES

PREPARATION 5 MINUTES

1 daikon
salt

Serves 4

Daikon, also known as mooli, is a long white root that you can buy at many large supermarkets. It's actually a kind of radish, and has a pleasantly peppery taste and very crisp texture. If you slice it thinly into rounds, it makes beautiful crisps. Other vegetables such as firm cauliflower, turnips or kohlrabi can be prepared in the same way, but daikon is particularly effective because of its shape.

1 Peel or scrub the daikon, then cut into thin slices.

2 Serve straight away, sprinkled with a little salt if you like.

1.0g carbs and 0g protein for the whole quantity

chunky avocado and coriander dip *v*

PHASES ① ② ③

1 lime
2 tablespoons chopped
   coriander leaves
1 large avocado
1 garlic clove, crushed
   (optional)
chilli powder, to taste
salt and freshly ground
   black pepper
paprika, to garnish

Serves 4

PREPARATION 10 MINUTES

This dip is quick to make, creamy and luxurious yet with a refreshing tang. Perfect with vegetable crudités.

1 Scrub the lime then, using a vegetable peeler, peel off a few pieces of rind and snip or cut them into shreds to make about a tablespoonful. Set aside. Squeeze the juice from the lime and put it into a large bowl with the chopped coriander.

2 Remove the peel and stone from the avocado, cut into rough chunks and put into the bowl. Add the garlic, if using, then mash all the ingredients together lightly with a fork, to produce a creamy mixture.

3 Season with salt, pepper and chilli powder to taste. Spoon the mixture into a small bowl and garnish with a sprinkling of paprika and the lime rind.

2.7g carbs and 1.8g protein per serving

courgette chips

PHASES 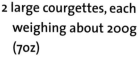 1 2 3

PREPARATION 5 MINUTES • **COOKING** 35 MINUTES

2 large courgettes, each weighing about 200g (7oz)
2 egg whites
¼ teaspoon cream of tartar
55g (2oz) ground almonds
55g (2oz) finely grated dry Parmesan cheese
a little cayenne pepper (optional)

Makes 16

These crisp and crunchy 'chips' are good as a snack, on their own, or with a creamy dip.

1 Preheat the oven to 230°C/450°F/Gas 8. Line a baking sheet with baking parchment.

2 Cut each courgette in half lengthways and then in half again to make four long pieces. Then slice each piece in half horizontally, so that you have 16 quite chunky chips in total.

3 Whisk the egg whites with the cream of tartar until very stiff – so that you could turn the bowl upside down without them falling out.

4 Dip the courgette chips first in the egg white, to coat them as well as you can, and then into either the ground almonds or the grated Parmesan cheese – or into both! Sprinkle with a little cayenne pepper, if you like, and place them on the baking sheet.

5 Bake for about 10–12 minutes, or until they are golden brown and crisp. Serve hot, warm or cold.

16.1g carbs and 44.2g protein for the whole quantity
1.0g carbs and 2.8g protein per 'chip'

tofu crisps *v*

PHASES

PREPARATION 5 MINUTES • **COOKING** 10 MINUTES

250g (9oz) packet tofu,
   drained
oil, for shallow-frying
salt
flavourings, as desired,
   such as salt and vinegar,
   garlic or onion salt,
   paprika, dried herb
   mixes

Makes 250g (9oz)

If you cut tofu into really thin slices and fry them in oil until they are golden brown, they are almost like crisps. Once fried, you can toss them in different flavourings: salt and vinegar, garlic or onion salt, paprika or dried herb mixes. And you can use smoked tofu for 'bacon' flavour crisps.

1 Cut the tofu into very thin slices, like crisps.

2 Fry the tofu in 1cm (½in) oil in a frying pan until crisp and golden on one side, then turn them over and cook the other side. You may need to do them in two batches, depending on the size of your frying pan, because it is important for them to have enough room to cook evenly.

3 Drain the crisps on kitchen paper – the first batch will keep perfectly well while you do the rest. Toss them all with a little salt and the flavouring of your choice and serve as soon as possible. They will keep crisp for about an hour but get rather leathery after that, so don't do them too far in advance.

2.5g carbs and 40g protein for the whole batch

cheese crackers

PHASES

225g (8oz) Cheddar
cheese, finely grated

Makes 24

These are easy to make and yummy to eat. You do need to cook them on baking parchment or you'll never get them off the tin! (You can get this paper at any supermarket.) And I would recommend that you choose a well-flavoured Cheddar for the best possible results!

1 Preheat the oven to 200°C/400°F/Gas 6. Cover a large baking sheet with baking parchment.

2 Put little piles of grated cheese on the paper, allowing room around each for spreading. You will probably have to do them in several batches.

3 Bake for about 8–10 minutes, or until they are golden brown and when you try to lift one off the paper it feels firm. If it is bendy and collapses, pop them back in the oven for a minute or two longer and test again.

4 Cool on the paper, then lift off with a spatula and serve with dips. They keep well in an airtight container.

> **3.2g carbs and 56.8g protein for the whole quantity**
> **negligible carbs and 2.4g protein per crisp**

fried, braised and grilled meals

THE RECIPES IN THIS chapter can be speedily made on top of the stove or under the grill. There are some quick cheese dishes, a couple of very tasty ways with tofu, and one recipe – Vegetarian Steaks Braised in Red Wine – that uses a quick version of the Japanese food, seitan, which is made from gluten powder, although tofu or Quorn fillets are equally successful used instead to make an excellent main course.

Some of these recipes are suitable for the barbecue, especially the Ricotta Rissoles, the Grilled Courgette with Halloumi Cheese, the Grilled Fennel with Radicchio and Garlic Cream, and the Sandwiched Tofu with Soy Sauce.

To accompany the main dishes, cooked green vegetables or a salad are quick to prepare and low in carbs, and they go well with all of the recipes. Look at the chapter on Side Vegetables (pages 122–9) for more ideas. When you are keeping the meal low-carb, potatoes are out, but creamy mashed cauliflower or turnips make a light and creamy substitute, and roasted cauliflower or turnips can take the place of roast potatoes.

Although low in carbs, the dishes in this chapter will also appeal to people who aren't into low-carbing – just serve their portion with potatoes or whatever accompaniments they want, to complete the meal.

spicy tofu

PHASES ❶ ❷ ❸

1 tablespoon paprika
1 teaspoon ground cumin
1 teaspoon ground
   coriander
½ teaspoon sea salt
250g (9oz) packet tofu,
   drained
1 tablespoon olive oil
2 tablespoons lemon juice
freshly ground black
   pepper

Serves 2

PREPARATION 5 MINUTES • **COOKING** 15 MINUTES

Fried tofu is always tasty, and here it is first covered with some piquant spices making it very good indeed.

1 Mix the paprika, cumin, coriander, salt and a grinding of black pepper on a plate and spread it out.

2 Cut the tofu in half, then slice each half horizontally to make four pieces. Dip the pieces into the spices, coating them all over.

3 Heat the oil in a frying pan, add the tofu and cook until brown and crispy on one side, about 4–5 minutes. Turn the pieces over and cook the other side.

4 Pour in the lemon juice. Let the mixture sizzle and bubble until the liquid disappears, then serve at once.

3.8g carbs and 21.7g protein per serving

vegetarian steaks
braised in red wine

PHASES ❷ ❸

PREPARATION 25 MINUTES • COOKING 45 MINUTES

4 tablespoons olive oil
1 medium onion, thinly
    sliced
1 garlic clove, crushed
150g (5½oz) small white
    mushrooms, sliced
28g (1oz) butter or vegan
    margarine
150ml (¼ pint) red wine
salt and freshly ground
    black pepper
chopped parsley, to
    garnish

For the seitan
100g (3½oz) gluten
    powder
1 tablespoon soy sauce
4–6 tablespoons water

For the stock
425ml (¾ pint) water
1 teaspoon vegetable
    bouillon stock powder

Serves 2, makes about
325g (11½oz) of seitan

The steaks are made from wheat protein called seitan.
I explained the easy way to make this in *The Vegetarian
Low-Carb Diet* and it's so useful that I'm repeating it here.
Once made, you can use the seitan in many ways: as a meat-
replacement in stews and casseroles (you could use it to make
the Goulash, Thai Curry with Cauliflower and Quick Asparagus,
Quorn and Red Pepper Stir-fry given in this book) or even
cooked and then ground up and made into burgers. Also, once
it has been simmered in the stock, it can be drained and
frozen for future use. Here, it is braised.

Traditionally in Japan, seitan was made by rinsing the starch
of ordinary wheat flour, just leaving the protein-rich gluten.
You can still make it like this but a quick and easy alternative
is simply to mix up some gluten powder. (For details about
where to obtain gluten powder see Sources and Stockists on
page 150.) The braise would also work superbly with ready-
bought Quorn fillets.

1 To make the seitan, put the gluten powder into a bowl. Add
   the soy sauce and enough water to mix to a dough; it will
   become springy and bouncy almost immediately.

2 Knead for 1–2 minutes, stretch it flat with your hands, then
   fold and roll it. Flatten it again. With a sharp knife, cut it into
   pieces of the size you want – largish, steak-like pieces are
   best for this recipe. The pieces will swell as they cook.

3 Make a quick stock by heating the 425ml (¾ pint) water and the bouillon powder. When it boils, add the seitan pieces, cover and simmer for 30 minutes. Drain thoroughly. The seitan is now ready for use (or you can freeze it at this stage for future use).

4 To make the braise, heat half the oil in a deep frying pan. Add the onion and cook for about 10 minutes, or until tender and golden. Stir in the garlic and mushrooms and cook for 2–3 minutes, then remove the onions and garlic from the pan and transfer to a plate temporarily.

5 Add the rest of the oil and the butter or vegan margarine to the frying pan, put in the seitan and fry on both sides until golden brown. Put the onion and garlic back in the pan with the red wine and some seasoning. Bring to the boil then let it simmer away for a few minutes, or until most of the red wine has disappeared, leaving just some shiny gravy. Scatter with chopped parsley and serve at once.

> **11.7g carbs and 76g protein for the whole quantity of seitan, or 3.6g carbs and 24.4g protein for 100g (3½oz). The braise contains 11.4g carbs and 6.3g protein per serving.**

sandwiched tofu with soy sauce

PHASES ① ② ③

250g (9oz) plain tofu, drained
2 tablespoons peanut butter
soya flour or non-GMO soya protein isolate powder, for coating
olive oil, for shallow-frying
soy sauce, to serve

Makes 2 'sandwiches'

PREPARATION 10 MINUTES • **COOKING** 10 MINUTES

Very quick to make, rich in protein and low in carbs, these nutty sandwiches are great for a snack and can also be jazzed up as a main course if you serve them with some steamed pak choy, fried baby mushrooms and a garnish of chopped fresh coriander.

1 Cut the tofu to give you four thin pieces that you can sandwich together in pairs.

2 Make two sandwiches of the tofu by spreading the slices with the peanut butter and pressing them together.

3 Dip the sandwiches in soy protein powder then shallow-fry them in olive oil until crisp on both sides. Serve with soy sauce for dipping.

7.5g carbs and 26g protein per 'sandwich' (using soya flour; if using soya protein isolate powder reduce carbs and increase protein accordingly).

grilled courgette with halloumi cheese

PHASES

PREPARATION 10 MINUTES • **COOKING** 10 MINUTES

4 medium courgettes
450g (1lb) halloumi cheese
olive oil, for brushing
lemon slices, to serve

Serves 4

You can get halloumi cheese at large supermarkets. You need to read the packets, because some batches are made with animal rennet and some are not. Halloumi cheese keeps for months in the refrigerator and it also freezes. Celery and Tomato Salsa goes well with this.

1 Cut the courgettes into slices about 5mm (¼in) thick. Cut the halloumi cheese into similar slices.

2 Brush the courgette slices on both sides with olive oil. Either cook them under a hot grill until lightly browned and tender, or, if you have a griddle, cook them on that – they look attractive with the grid-marks on them.

3 While the courgette is cooking, fry the halloumi slices in a dry frying pan until golden brown, turning to cook both sides. They cook very quickly, just a minute or so on each side.

4 Serve the halloumi with the courgette and the lemon slices.

6.5g carbs and 25g protein per serving

grilled fennel with radicchio and garlic cream

PHASES

PREPARATION 15 MINUTES • **COOKING** 30 MINUTES

2 fennel bulbs
1 radicchio
olive oil
salt and freshly ground
   black pepper
lemon slices or fresh herb
   sprigs, to garnish

For the garlic cream

150g (5½oz) Boursin garlic
   and herb cream cheese
   or vegan herb and garlic
   cream cheese
3–4 tablespoons hot water

Serves 2

Fennel and radicchio are delectable barbecued or grilled and served with this creamy sauce.

1 The garlic cream can be made in advance and kept in a covered dish in the refrigerator. To make it, simply mash the garlic cream cheese to break it up and beat in 3–4 tablespoons of hot water to make a smooth, creamy mixture.

2 Trim the fennel and radicchio, removing any tough leaves and pieces of stem but leaving enough of the stem to hold the leaves together at the base. Cut each down through the stem into halves, then into quarters and eighths, so that they are still joined together at the base, if possible. Steam or parboil the fennel for about 8 minutes, or until it is just tender without being at all soggy. Drain well and dry with kitchen paper.

3 Brush both the fennel and the radicchio with oil and sprinkle with some salt and pepper, then grill them until they are lightly charred on both sides: this will take about 5–8 minutes on a barbecue and slightly longer, about 15 minutes, under a conventional grill.

4 Serve hot or warm, garnished with lemon slices or fresh herb sprigs, accompanied by the garlic cream sauce.

17.4g carbs and 3.6g protein per serving

vegan variation

Use vegan garlic and herb cream cheese – remember to count the carbs.

ricotta rissoles

PHASES ❷ ❸

500g (1lb 2oz) ricotta cheese
2 tablespoons chopped fresh herbs, such as chives, dill, parsley and chervil
55g (2oz) ready-grated Parmesan cheese
1 tablespoon soya flour
1 egg
2 tablespoons olive oil
salt and freshly ground black pepper

Serves 4

PREPARATION 15 MINUTES, PLUS OPTIONAL CHILLING TIME
COOKING 5 MINUTES

These light rissoles are good with a crisp leafy or tomato salad. They need to be eaten as soon as they are cooked as they tend to collapse if kept hot under the grill or in the oven.

1 Put the ricotta cheese into a bowl and mix in the chopped herbs, Parmesan cheese, soya flour, egg, and salt and freshly ground black pepper.

2 Divide the mixture into eight pieces and form into rissoles. Chill until just before you want to serve them.

3 Heat the olive oil in a frying pan – preferably non-stick – and put in the rissoles. Fry them for 1–2 minutes, or until they are crisp and golden brown on one side. Carefully turn them over and fry them until the other side, too, is crisp and golden brown, and the inside has heated through. Serve immediately with salad.

7.5g carbs and 21g protein per serving

fried pumpkin with deep-fried sage

PHASES

PREPARATION 15 MINUTES • COOKING 15 MINUTES

a little oil, for deep frying
12 sprigs of fresh sage
600g (1lb 5oz) pumpkin, weighed with skin and seeds
4 garlic cloves, peeled
3–4 tablespoons olive oil
Maldon salt
freshly grated Parmesan cheese (optional)

Serves 4

Thinly sliced pumpkin, fried in olive oil until it is crisp on the outside, tender within, makes a quick, good starter. The crisp, deep-fried sage makes an attractive garnish, and is quick to do – but you could equally well use fresh sprigs. I have suggested using Maldon salt here because it is a particularly tasty, flaked sea salt that you can crumble with your fingers, but any sea salt would work well.

1 First prepare the deep-fried sage for the garnish. Heat 2.5cm (1in) oil in a small saucepan. When it is sizzling hot, put in some of the sage sprigs and deep-fry for 1–2 minutes, until they are crunchy, then drain them on kitchen paper and repeat the process with the remainder. Keep on one side until required.

2 Peel the skin from the piece of pumpkin and remove the seeds and threads. Cut the flesh into long, slim pieces about 10cm (4in) by 2.5–4cm (1–1½in), and not more than 5mm (¼in) thick.

3 Crush the garlic to a paste with some salt. With a knife, smear this garlic paste very thinly on each side of the pumpkin slices to flavour them lightly.

4 Heat the olive oil in a frying pan, and fry the pumpkin slices for about 3 minutes on each side, or until they are lightly browned and crisp, and feel tender when pierced with the point of a knife. Remove from the pan and drain them on kitchen paper.

5 Serve as soon as possible on warmed plates, sprinkled with a little crunchy Maldon salt and garnished with the deep-fried sage. Hand round the Parmesan cheese separately, if you like.

7.6g carbs and 1.3g protein per serving (not including Parmesan)

green peppers stuffed with cauliflower cheese

PHASES

PREPARATION 15 MINUTES • **COOKING** 30 MINUTES

4 medium green peppers
1 medium cauliflower,
   in small florets
200g (7oz) Cheddar
   cheese, grated
salt and freshly ground
   black pepper

Serves 4

Strong-flavoured Cheddar cheese is perfect for these quick, easy and very tasty stuffed peppers.

1 Halve the peppers, cutting through their stems. Carefully remove the white inner part and seeds, keeping the stem intact. Place on a grill pan, shiny-side up, and grill for about 10–15 minutes, or until tender.

2 Cook the cauliflower in 2.5cm (1in) of boiling water, covered, for 4–5 minutes, or until just tender. Drain and mix with half the cheese and some salt and pepper.

3 Fill each pepper with the cauliflower cheese mixture, dividing it between them, sprinkle the rest of the cheese on top and grill for about 10 minutes, or until the cheese is melting, bubbling and golden brown. Serve at once.

10.7g carbs and 17.0g protein per serving

stuffed courgettes with fresh tomato sauce

PHASES

PREPARATION 25 MINUTES • COOKING 30 MINUTES

4 plump courgettes, each
about 125g (4½oz)
2 × 150g (5½oz) Boursin
cheese with garlic and
herbs
sprigs of fresh dill to
garnish

For the sauce

1 small onion, peeled and
finely chopped
1 tablespoon olive oil
450g (1lb) tomatoes,
quartered
salt and freshly ground
black pepper

Serves 4

These light and summery courgettes, filled with herby cheese and grilled until golden, are good served with some French beans.

1 To make the sauce, fry the onion in the oil in a saucepan for 5 minutes without browning. Add the tomatoes, cover and cook for 10–15 minutes, or until the tomatoes have collapsed. Liquidise, sieve and season.

2 Halve the courgettes and cook in 2.5cm (1in) of boiling water until just tender. Drain very well. Scoop out the seeds with a pointed teaspoon or a knife.

3 Place the courgettes in a shallow casserole or grill pan. Fill each cavity with the cream cheese, moistened with a little hot water, if necessary.

4 Place under a hot grill until heated through and lightly browned. Garnish with fresh dill sprigs and serve with the tomato sauce.

7.5g carbs and 4.1g protein per serving

vegan variation
Use vegan herb and garlic cream cheese – remember to check the carbs.

deep-fried camembert

PHASES

PREPARATION 10 MINUTES • **COOKING** 10 MINUTES

1 × 250g (9oz) Camembert
   in individual portions
2 eggs, beaten
40g (1½oz) dry grated
   Parmesan cheese

Serves 2

This delicious treat can be low-carb if you use dry grated Parmesan cheese to coat the Camembert instead of the usual breadcrumbs. Make sure the cheese is very dry: grate it in advance and leave it uncovered for a few hours to dry out – and be sure to coat the Camembert very thoroughly so that it doesn't leak out when you fry it. If you want something sweet with this, try the Red Pepper Sauce on page 64.

1 Dip each portion of Camembert into the beaten eggs then into the Parmesan, making sure each one is completely coated (this can be done in advance). Chill the Camembert in the refrigerator until about 5 minutes before you want to serve the meal.

2 Deep-fry the Camembert in oil heated to 180–190°C (350–375°F), or until a cube of bread dropped into the hot oil becomes golden brown in 1 minute. Let the cheese fry for about 5 minutes, or until it is golden brown and crisp all over. Remove with a slotted spoon, place on kitchen paper and blot off any excess oil. Serve immediately.

1.7g carbs and 38.9g protein per serving

curries, casseroles and stir-fries

THE RECIPES IN THIS chapter are surprisingly quick and easy to make, in spite of the longer lists of ingredients you will find for some of them. Some of them contain protein in the form of Quorn, TVP (textured vegetable protein) chunks or tofu – for more information about all of these protein foods, see pages 14–17. Others, for example the Spiced Pumpkin, Okra and Baby Sweetcorn Casserole, and the Ragoût of Wild Mushrooms, are purely vegetable based, and need the addition of protein to make a complete meal.

One way of adding protein to a dish is to serve it with grated cheese, chopped hardboiled eggs or a side dish of spicy tofu; or, for the type of dishes in this chapter, a protein-rich rice replacement can work well. You can make this from natural TVP 'mince', which you can buy at health stores. Just hydrate it by soaking briefly and simmering in water, then drain, toss with a little butter or olive oil, and season. This does not taste quite like rice, of course, but it's bland and slightly chewy and soaks up the juices of a curry or stew well.

Another way to add protein is to have a protein-rich starter or pudding – there are plenty of choose from, but I think a piece of homemade low-carb cheesecake always goes down well.

goulash ⓥ

PREPARATION 15 MINUTES • **COOKING** 35 MINUTES

1 tablespoon olive oil
1 small onion, sliced
1 small green pepper,
    chopped
175g (6oz) Quorn chunks,
    or TVP chunks (hydrated
    weight), or plain tofu
    cubes
1 garlic clove, crushed
½ teaspoon paprika
½ × 400g (14oz) can
    chopped tomatoes in
    juice
125ml (4 fl oz) water
1 teaspoon vegetable
    bouillon stock powder
½ teaspoon oregano
1 teaspoon tomato purée
salt and freshly ground
    black pepper
chopped fresh parsley,
    to garnish
soured cream (optional),
    to serve

Serves 2

The main ingredient in this richly flavoured dish is Quorn, which is high in protein and quite low in carbs, as explained in the section on Quorn on page 16. If you want a vegan version, simply make it with either dried TVP chunks, which you can buy at health stores, or with tofu. (If you use TVP, soak to hydrate before use, following directions on the packet.) Some cauliflower 'rice' (page 98) or 'mash' (pages 120–1) would go well with this.

1 Heat the oil in a large frying pan, add the onion and pepper, and cook for 5 minutes. Add the Quorn, hydrated TVP or tofu and cook for a further 5 minutes, stirring from time to time to prevent sticking.

2 Add the garlic and paprika. Stir for a few seconds, then stir in the tomatoes, water, bouillon, oregano and tomato purée.

3 Bring to the boil and simmer for about 25 minutes, or until the sauce is thick. Season with salt and pepper.

4 Serve at once, swirled with soured cream, if liked, and scattered with chopped parsley.

13.7g carbs and 14.8g protein per serving made with Quorn (lower with alternative proteins), soured cream extra, refer to carton

vegetable curry with coriander raita

PHASES ② ③

PREPARATION 30 MINUTES • **COOKING** 35 MINUTES

1 onion, peeled and
  chopped
4 tablespoons olive oil
walnut-sized piece of
  fresh root ginger, grated
4 garlic cloves, crushed
½ teaspoon turmeric
2 teaspoons ground
  coriander
2 teaspoons ground cumin
1 small cauliflower, in
  florets
225g (8oz) French beans,
  halved
225g (8oz) courgettes,
  sliced
1 × 400g (14oz) can
  chopped tomatoes
1 teaspoon garam masala
salt and freshly ground
  black pepper

For the TVP 'rice'
175g (6oz) TVP (textured
  vegetable protein)
  natural 'mince'
1 tablespoon olive oil

This recipe uses cauliflower, but any root vegetables can be used for this warming winter dish: carrots, kohlrabi, celeriac or parsnips. This curry is one of those dishes that tastes even better the next day after the flavours have had a chance to develop thoroughly. Serve with the coriander raita and TVP 'rice'.

1 Fry the onion in the olive oil in a large saucepan for about 10 minutes, or until tender.

2 Stir in the ginger, garlic, turmeric, coriander and cumin, and cook for 1–2 minutes, then add the cauliflower, French beans and courgettes.

3 Cook for another 2–3 minutes, then add the tomatoes. Bring to the boil, cover and cook gently for 15–20 minutes, or until all the vegetables are tender. Stir in the garam masala and season to taste.

4 To prepare the TVP 'rice', simmer the TVP in water to cover until tender – about 15 minutes. Drain off any excess water. Add the olive oil and season to taste.

For the raita

300ml (½ pint) Greek or
plain soya yogurt
3–4 tablespoons chopped
fresh coriander

Serves 4

5 Make the raita by mixing together the yogurt and coriander.
Add seasoning to taste.

6 Serve the curry with the TVP rice and raita.

11.8g carbs and 4.3g protein per serving of curry
5.1g carbs and 21.3g protein per serving of rice
3.5g carbs and 3.0g protein per serving of raita

spiced pumpkin, okra and baby sweetcorn casserole (V)

PHASES (2) (3)

225g (8oz) okra
1kg (2lb 4oz) pumpkin,
 weighed with skin and
 seeds
4 tablespoons olive oil
1 onion, peeled and
 chopped
2 garlic cloves, crushed
1 cinnamon stick
225g (8oz) baby sweetcorn
1 × 400g (14oz) can
 chopped tomatoes in
 juice
salt and freshly ground
 black pepper

Serves 4

PREPARATION 20 MINUTES • **COOKING** 35 MINUTES

Pumpkin makes a perfect base for this lovely casserole for chilly days. Serve with TVP 'rice' (page 94) or grated cheese for extra protein. Or follow with a yummy protein-rich pudding like Strawberry Cheesecake (pages 136–7).

1 Prepare the okra by cutting away the stalk and cap using a sharp knife, being careful not to cut into the pod and exposing the seeds (this will ensure the okra cooks without making the sauce thick). Remove the peel, seeds and threads from the pumpkin and cut the flesh into fairly thin slices.

2 Heat the oil in a large saucepan and put in the onion. Cover and cook for 5 minutes, then add the garlic, pumpkin and cinnamon stick, broken in two. Stir well, then cover again and cook for a further 10 minutes.

3 Add the okra, sweetcorn and tomatoes. Season with salt and pepper, cover and leave to cook for 20 minutes, or until the vegetables are all tender. Check the seasoning and serve.

23.2g carbs and 5.5g protein per serving

ragoût of wild mushrooms

PHASES

1kg (2lb 4oz) wild
   mushrooms
4 tablespoons olive oil
3 garlic cloves, crushed
4 tablespoons double or
   soya cream
lemon juice
salt and freshly ground
   black pepper
chopped fresh parsley,
   preferably flat-leaf,
   to garnish

Serves 4

PREPARATION 10 MINUTES • **COOKING** 20 MINUTES

This tasty ragoût is wonderful made with wild mushrooms, but a mixture of oyster, button and shiitake mushrooms also works well. Turnip Gratin Dauphinois (page 127) is great with this.

1 Quickly rinse the wild mushrooms and pat dry with kitchen paper. Slice them. Heat the olive oil in a pan and cook the mushrooms and garlic over a moderate heat, uncovered, until they are tender and any liquid they make has bubbled away. The time varies according to the type of mushroom; it can be as little as 5 minutes, or as long as 20, but if you test the mushrooms with a sharp knife you will be able to tell when they are tender.

2 Add the cream, a squeeze of lemon juice and some salt and pepper to season. Get the mixture really hot, sprinkle with parsley then serve at once.

6.5g carbs and 8.2g protein per serving

thai curry with cauliflower 'rice'

PHASES

PREPARATION 15 MINUTES • **COOKING** 10–15 MINUTES

2 tablespoons olive oil

350g (12oz) Quorn chunks, or TVP chunks (hydrated weight), or plain tofu cubes

4 spring onions, roughly chopped

1 tablespoon Thai curry paste

1 × 400ml (14 fl oz) can coconut milk

salt and freshly ground black pepper

chopped fresh coriander, to garnish

For the cauliflower 'rice'

1 large cauliflower, about 600g (1lb 5z)

Serves 4

This is an easy Thai curry to make using commercial Thai curry paste. I used a supermarket own brand of red curry paste that is vegetarian, but always read the label before you buy, as many are not. This is very rich so something bland or fresh goes well with it, such as the cauliflower 'rice' described below, or simply some steamed broccoli or pak choy. (If you prefer a less-rich version, replace half the coconut milk with water.)

1 Heat the oil in a large saucepan. Put in the Quorn, TVP or Tofu and fry for 2–3 minutes, or until golden.

2 Add the spring onions, curry paste and coconut milk, and season with salt and pepper. Leave to cook gently for 5–10 minutes.

3 Meanwhile make the cauliflower 'rice'. Grate the cauliflower finely, or chop it in a food processor, so that it looks like rice. Cook in 2.5cm (1in) of boiling water for 2–3 minutes, or until tender. Drain well and season to taste with salt.

4 Scatter the chopped coriander over the top of the curry and serve with the cauliflower rice.

cauliflower rice has 5g carbs and 3g protein per serving; the curry has 8.4g carbs and 28.7g protein per serving

quick asparagus, quorn and red pepper stir-fry

PHASES

225g (8oz) trimmed
asparagus cut into 5cm
(2in) lengths

2 tablespoons olive oil

175g (6oz) Quorn chunks,
or TVP chunks (hydrated
weight), or plain tofu
cubes

2 tablespoons soy sauce

1 teaspoon grated fresh
root ginger

1 garlic clove, crushed

pinch of dried red chilli
flakes

1 large red pepper,
deseeded and thinly
sliced

4 spring onions, chopped

salt and freshly ground
black pepper

cauliflower 'rice', to serve
(optional)

Serves 2

PREPARATION 15 MINUTES • **COOKING** 10 MINUTES

This stir-fry is full of flavour using tender young asparagus and ripe red pepper, and it can be served with cauliflower 'rice' (page 98) for a tasty and filling meal. Remember to use one of the alternatives if you want a vegan version. For more about Quorn, see the reference section on page 16.

1 Cook the asparagus in boiling water to cover for about 2 minutes, or until par-cooked but still crunchy. Drain and set aside.

2 Heat the oil in a large saucepan or wok. Put in the Quorn, TVP or Tofu and fry for 2–3 minutes, or until golden. Add the soy sauce, ginger, garlic and chilli flakes. Stir-fry for 1–2 minutes to mix in the flavourings.

3 Add the red pepper, spring onions and asparagus, and stir-fry for a further 2–3 minutes, or until the red pepper is slightly softened and everything is hot.

4 Season with salt and pepper, then serve with the cauliflower rice, if you like.

> **13.4g carbs and 16.6g protein per serving made with Quorn (fewer carbs if using tofu); add on 5g carbs and 3g protein per portion if serving the cauliflower rice**

cabbage, mushroom and peanut stir-fry Ⓥ

PHASES ② ③

PREPARATION 20 MINUTES • **COOKING** 15 MINUTES

1 tablespoon toasted
sesame oil
1 Chinese cabbage,
shredded
250g (9oz) button or
chestnut mushrooms,
sliced
3 garlic cloves, finely
chopped or sliced
2 tablespoons peanut
butter
1 tablespoon soy sauce
salt and freshly ground
black pepper
dash of Tabasco sauce
(optional)

Serves 2

With the addition of a few simple ingredients, Chinese cabbage (sometimes called 'Chinese leaves' in the supermarket or 'napa cabbage' in the US) can be turned into a quick and tasty meal. Use an organic peanut butter without additional sweeteners: the best ones consist only of peanuts and salt. This is filling and delicious just as it is, and perfect for a low-carber; for others, serve it with rice.

1 Heat the oil in a large saucepan or wok.

2 Add the cabbage, mushrooms and garlic. Stir-fry for about 5 minutes, or until the cabbage is tender.

3 Add the peanut butter and soy sauce to the pan and stir gently until the peanut butter has melted and all the leaves are coated.

4 Season with salt, pepper and a dash of Tabasco sauce, if you like, and serve.

8g carbs and 10g protein per serving

'pasta' dishes

AH, PASTA! BY NO STRETCH of the imagination can normal pasta fit into the low-carb diet, but there are alternatives. If you crave macaroni cheese, make the Mockeroni Cheese, which really seems to hit the 'pasta-bake' spot for many low-carbers. And both the Cabbage Cannelloni and the Omelette Cannelloni with Spinach Filling have similar appeal although with different flavours (the Cabbage Cannelloni can also be vegan).

When it comes to spaghetti and other pasta replacements, spaghetti marrow, or squash, which has spaghetti-like fibres when cooked, can be served in very similar ways to spaghetti; here it is cooked with a Dolcelatte cream and walnuts. I also like to cut vegetables into pasta-like strips, cook them lightly and serve them with pasta sauces. They don't taste like pasta – although you can use your favourite low-carb pasta sauces such as pesto or a creamy cheese sauce – but they are tasty dishes in their own right.

If you can find a low-carb pasta substitute in the shops it would be worth a try if you can track some down. There is also a type of noodle that is made wholly from soya (and therefore low-carb) that can be bought from Asian shops.

fettuccini of summer vegetables

PHASES

PREPARATION 15 MINUTES • **COOKING** 5 MINUTES

225g (8oz) green cabbage
225g (8oz) courgettes
225g (8oz) asparagus,
   trimmed and halved
1 tablespoon olive oil
125g (4½oz) shaved
   Parmesan cheese
salt and freshly ground
   black pepper

Serves 2

Cabbage and courgettes can be sliced very thinly to look like pasta, and the addition of asparagus makes a tasty combination. This is a quick and easy 'pasta' dish simply tossed in olive oil and served with Parmesan cheese.

1 Cut the cabbage and courgettes into long, thin fettuccini-like strips.

2 Bring half a saucepanful of water to the boil, put in the courgettes, then the cabbage and asparagus. Cook for about 4 minutes, or until the vegetables are just tender.

3 Drain the vegetables and return them to the pan. Add the olive oil, some salt and freshly ground black pepper and serve with the shaved Parmesan cheese.

9.8g carbs and 26.2g protein per serving

cabbage tagliatelle with cream cheese and mushroom sauce

PHASES

450g (1lb) cabbage such
   as January King or
   Sweetheart
125g (4½oz) button
   mushrooms, sliced
1 tablespoon olive oil
75g (2¾oz) Boursin cream
   cheese with garlic and
   herbs
salt and freshly ground
   black pepper

Serves 2

PREPARATION 20 MINUTES • **COOKING** 15 MINUTES

In this recipe, cabbage is treated like tagliatelle and served with a creamy sauce with garlic and herbs. It's quick and yummy.

1. Shred the cabbage into fine, long strips, like tagliatelle.

2. Cook in boiling water, covered, for about 4 minutes, or until just done.

3. Fry the mushrooms in the olive oil for 3–4 minutes, or until tender.

4. Drain the cabbage and add to the pan with the mushrooms. Stir in the Boursin and a little salt and freshly ground black pepper to taste. Serve immediately.

8.2g carbs and 7g protein per serving

vegan variation

Use vegan garlic and herb cheese – remember to check the carbs.

spaghetti squash with dolcelatte cream and walnuts

PHASES

PREPARATION 15 MINUTES • **COOKING** 40 MINUTES

450g (1lb) spaghetti
   squash
28g (1oz) butter
150ml (¼ pint) double
   cream
125g (4½oz) Dolcelatte
   cheese
55g (2oz) walnuts, roughly
   chopped
salt and freshly ground
   black pepper
freshly grated Parmesan
   cheese, to serve

Serves 2

Spaghetti squash makes a great pasta substitute, especially when mixed with cream and exquisitely flavoured Dolcelatte cheese.

1. Bring a large saucepan of water to the boil; it needs to be large enough to hold the squash whole. Prick the squash in a few places, then put it into the saucepan. Cover and boil for 30 minutes, or until it's tender when pierced with a skewer.

2. Drain the squash and, holding it with a cloth, halve it and scoop out the 'spaghetti' into a hot saucepan. Add the butter, cream, Dolcelatte, and some salt and pepper to taste.

3. Stir quickly over a gentle heat, just to distribute all the ingredients. Transfer to warmed serving plates. Scatter over the walnuts, sprinkle with Parmesan and serve at once.

15.8g carbs and 10.8g protein per serving

vegan variation

Omit the Dolcelatte; use vegan garlic and herb cream cheese, soya cream and vegan Parmesan. Remember to check the carbs.

omelette cannelloni with spinach filling

PHASES

PREPARATION 20 MINUTES • **COOKING** 40 MINUTES

750g (1lb 10oz) spinach
125g (4½oz) low-fat cream
   cheese
8 tablespoons freshly
   grated Parmesan
freshly grated nutmeg
4 eggs
2 tablespoons water
1 tablespoon olive oil
salt and freshly ground
   black pepper

Serves 4

Light omelettes make a fantastic low-carb cannelloni to be filled with fresh spinach and cream cheese. Parmesan and nutmeg give the filling a good, strong flavour.

1 Preheat the oven to 190°C/375°F/Gas 5.

2 Cook the spinach, with just the water that clings to it, in a large saucepan, covered, for 6–7 minutes, or until tender. Drain well and mix it with the cream cheese and half the Parmesan. Season with salt, pepper and grated nutmeg. Set aside.

3 Whisk the eggs with the water, and salt and pepper to taste. Brush a frying pan (preferably non-stick) with a little of the olive oil and heat it, then pour in enough of the egg – about 2 tablespoons – to make a small omelette; cook for a few seconds, until it is set, then lift it out onto a plate. Continue in this way until you have about eight small omelettes, piling them up on top of each other.

4 Spoon a little of the spinach mixture onto the edge of one of the omelettes and roll up; place in a shallow gratin dish. Fill the rest of the omelettes in the same way, until all the spinach mixture is used up, placing them side by side in the dish.

5 Sprinkle with the remaining Parmesan and bake for about 25 minutes, or until bubbling and golden brown on top.

5.7g carbs and 20g protein per serving

cabbage cannelloni

PHASES   PREPARATION 30 MINUTES • COOKING 60 MINUTES

1 cabbage, such as January
   King or Sweetheart
1 onion, peeled and
   chopped
2 tablespoons olive oil
1 garlic clove, crushed
½ × 400g (14oz) can
   tomatoes in juice
225g (8oz) button
   mushrooms, chopped
175g (6oz) Cheddar cheese,
   grated
55g (2oz) freshly grated
   Parmesan cheese
salt and freshly ground
   black pepper

Serves 2

For this recipe you need tender cabbage leaves that are big enough to make into parcels. Young spring cabbage is ideal. You won't need the heart, so you could try shredding it, then mixing it with mayonnaise, yogurt and a dash of lemon juice, to make a salad for another meal.

1 Preheat the oven to 200°C/400°F/Gas 6.

2 Bring half a large saucepanful of water to the boil. Meanwhile, remove and discard any very tough leaves from the cabbage, then carefully ease off any that seem reasonably large and tender, aiming for eight.

3 When the water boils, put in the cabbage leaves, pushing them down below water level. Cover and cook for 5 minutes or so, until they are tender but not soggy. Drain well, spread them out on kitchen paper and blot dry.

4 Fry the onion in the oil, covered, for 5 minutes, then add the garlic and cook for a further 5 minutes. Remove and set aside half the onion. Add the tomatoes to the pan and cook, uncovered, for about 15 minutes, or until they form a thick sauce. Season with salt and pepper.

5 Put the mushrooms into another pan with the reserved onion. Fry for about 5 minutes, or until the mushrooms are tender, then remove from the heat and add the grated Cheddar cheese. Mix well.

6 Put some of the mushroom mixture into the centre of each cabbage leaf. Fold over the sides, and roll each leaf up neatly. Place in a shallow ovenproof dish, pour the tomato sauce over and sprinkle the grated Parmesan cheese over the top in a fairly thick layer. Bake for 25–30 minutes, or until hot and bubbling, and the top is golden brown and crisp.

15.9g carbs and 40.2g protein per serving

vegan variation

Use vegan Cheddar-style cheese (check the carbs, which vary according to the make), and top with a scattering of vegan Parmesan cheese, which you can buy 'ready grated' in a tub.

mockeroni cheese

PHASES

PREPARATION 10 MINUTES • **COOKING** 45–60 MINUTES

2 × 250g (9oz) packets tofu, drained
225g (8oz) grated Cheddar cheese
2 eggs, beaten
4 tablespoons double or soya cream
cayenne pepper, to taste
dry mustard powder, to taste
2–3 tablespoons grated Parmesan cheese
salt and freshly ground black pepper

Serves 4

Made from tofu, 'Mockeroni' cheese has become a low-carb classic. Here is a particularly quick and delicious version, which tastes surprisingly like the real thing.

1 Preheat the oven to 180°C/350°F/Gas 4.

2 Make sure the tofu is as dry as possible by blotting well with kitchen paper. Then cut it into small strips, like macaroni, and put it into a bowl. Add the grated Cheddar cheese, eggs, cream and a dash of cayenne and dry mustard. Season with salt and pepper to taste.

3 Transfer to a greased, shallow casserole and scatter the Parmesan cheese over the top. Bake for 45–60 minutes, or until the top is well browned.

2.6g carbs and 35.7g protein per serving

bakes

YOU WILL HAVE TO switch the oven on for all the recipes in this chapter, which is why I have grouped them together – but that doesn't mean they are all time-consuming to make. Some are 'specials': a couple of brilliant tarts with melt-in-your-mouth low-carb almond pastry, a roulade, a wonderful savoury loaf consisting of layers of oyster mushrooms, which looks most attractive when it's sliced, and a shepherd's pie. These all take a little time and trouble, although they are not difficult, and are certainly worth the effort.

Alongside these are several dishes that are particularly quick to make: the Baby Squash with Sage, Cream and Gruyère almost comes into the category of 'fast food' it's so easy; other dishes are quick and tasty, including the Divine Cauliflower Bake, which really does live up to its name, Courgettes Parmesan, and Pumpkin and Goat's Cheese Gratin, to mention just three.

All of these dishes can be enjoyed by both low-carbers and 'normal' vegetarians (and some are suitable for vegans, too). While testing recipes for this book I served some of them when entertaining and no one realised that they were eating a low-carb meal! As I have said before, one of the joys of the low-carb way of losing weight is that the food tastes so good.

courgettes parmesan

PHASES

450g (1lb) courgettes,
   sliced into batons
55g (2oz) freshly grated
   Parmesan (but you can
   get away with ready
   grated)
salt and freshly ground
   black pepper

Serves 2

PREPARATION 10 MINUTES • **COOKING** 35 MINUTES

Sliced courgettes baked with cheese make a simple dish that tastes exceptionally good. I like it as a quick-and-easy main course, but it also makes an interesting first course baked in individual ramekins.

1 Preheat the oven to 200°C/400°F/Gas 6.

2 Cook the courgettes in water to cover for 2–3 minutes, or until just tender. Drain.

3 Put the courgettes into a shallow ovenproof dish and season to taste. Sprinkle the Parmesan cheese on top to cover. Bake for 20–30 minutes, or until the top is golden brown and crisp. Serve at once.

6.1g carbs and 12.8g protein per serving

broccoli and brie bake

PHASES

700g (1lb 9oz) broccoli, cut into small florets
350g (12oz) Brie
150ml (¼ pint) soya cream
75g (2¾oz) Parmesan cheese, grated
salt and freshly ground black pepper

Serves 4

PREPARATION 15 MINUTES • **COOKING** 25 MINUTES

In this richly flavoured bake, the Brie melts into the cream to form a creamy sauce. I like to use soya cream because it's low in carbs and unsaturated, but you could use single dairy cream (although check the carbs if you do).

1 Preheat the oven to 200°C/400°F/Gas 6.

2 Cook the broccoli in 2.5cm (1in) of boiling water, or in a steamer, for about 4–5 minutes, until just tender. Drain and transfer to a shallow casserole dish.

3 Cut up the Brie, including the rind, into fairly thin slices. Add it to the casserole, distributing it evenly over the broccoli. Pour over the cream and add salt and pepper. Mash the broccoli and Brie into the cream a little with a fork, then sprinkle the Parmesan cheese on top, to cover it evenly.

4 Bake for 15–20 minutes, or until bubbly, golden brown and crisp.

8.5g carbs and 31.3g protein per serving

spinach roulade with mozzarella and tomato filling

PHASES

PREPARATION 40 MINUTES • **COOKING** 20 MINUTES

450g (1lb) fresh spinach or
175g (6oz) frozen
15g (½oz) butter
4 eggs, separated
freshly grated nutmeg
4 tablespoons grated
Parmesan cheese
salt and freshly ground
black pepper
3–4 sprigs of fresh basil,
to garnish

For the filling

55g (2oz) cream cheese
2 × 150g (5½oz) mozzarella
cheese (packed in
water), drained and
thinly sliced
2 tomatoes, thinly sliced

Serves 4

Light and moist spinach roulade is a classic that's ideal for low-carbing. It's delectable and much easier to make than you might think.

1. Preheat the oven to 200°C/400°F/Gas 6. Line a 23 × 33cm (9 × 13in) Swiss roll tin with baking parchment, to extend up the sides a little.

2. If you are using fresh spinach, cook it for a few minutes, or until it is very tender, in a dry pan with only the water that clings to the leaves. Frozen spinach just needs thawing. In either case, drain the spinach into a colander and press it very well to extract as much water as possible.

3. Chop the spinach and mix with the butter, egg yolks and a seasoning of salt, freshly ground black pepper and nutmeg to make a smooth, creamy-looking purée – this can be done in a food processor if you prefer.

4. Whisk the egg whites until they form stiff peaks. Gently add the spinach mixture and carefully fold it into the egg whites.

5. Tip the mixture into the prepared tin, level the top and sprinkle with 2 tablespoons of the Parmesan. Bake for 10–12 minutes, or until the top is springy.

6. Remove from the oven and turn out onto a piece of baking parchment sprinkled with the remaining Parmesan. Peel the paper off the roulade.

7   Spread the roulade with a thin layer of cream cheese (moistened with a little hot water, if necessary), then put the mozzarella cheese and tomato slices on top.

8   Roll up the roulade, starting at one of the long ends. Garnish with the basil and serve.

6.2g carbs and 30g protein per serving

layered oyster mushroom loaf

PHASES ① ② ③

10g (¼oz) dried
   mushrooms, porcini or
   morels
55g (2oz) butter
600g (1lb 5oz) oyster
   mushrooms
1 garlic clove, crushed
2 eggs
150ml (¼ pint) soya cream
salt and freshly ground
   black pepper

Serves 4

PREPARATION 40 MINUTES, PLUS 1 HOUR SOAKING
COOKING 1 HOUR 10 MINUTES

This loaf is so pretty! It makes an attractive and unusual main dish, and is excellent served with the Tomato and Red Wine Sauce on page 62 and some seasonal vegetables such as the Braised Celery on page 123.

1 Preheat the oven to 160°C/325°F/Gas 3. Line a 450g (1lb) loaf tin with a piece of baking parchment to cover the base and extend up the short sides; grease the other sides. Put the dried mushrooms into a bowl and add boiling water to just cover them. Leave to soak for 1 hour.

2 Meanwhile, melt the butter in a large saucepan, add the oyster mushrooms and cook for about 20 minutes, uncovered, until they are very tender and have absorbed their liquid. Chop the soaked mushrooms and add them to the pan with their liquid. Add the garlic, and cook for a further few minutes, or until they are dry. Remove from the heat and season with salt and pepper.

3 Arrange the mushrooms in layers in the loaf tin. Whisk together the eggs and cream, then pour this custard into the loaf tin, gently moving the oyster mushrooms with a knife and tipping the tin, to make sure that the custard seeps down between all the layers.

4 Put the loaf tin into a roasting tin of boiling water and bake for about 40 minutes, or until the loaf is set and golden brown and a skewer inserted into the centre comes out clean.

5   Run a knife around the edges of the loaf to loosen it, then turn it out onto a warmed serving dish. This loaf cuts well both hot and cold, but you need to use a sharp, serrated knife.

6.7g carbs and 10.6g protein per serving

pumpkin and goat's cheese gratin

PHASES

900g (2lb) pumpkin, weighed with the skin and seeds
28g (1oz) butter
225g (8oz) firm goat's cheese log, cut into thin slices
55g (2oz) fresh Parmesan cheese, finely grated
salt and freshly ground black pepper

Serves 4

PREPARATION 30 MINUTES • **COOKING** 40 MINUTES

The sharp flavour of the goat's cheese contrasts well with the sweet creaminess of the pumpkin in this easy gratin. I like to serve it with the Bitterleaf Salad with Walnut Dressing (page 46).

1   Preheat the oven to 200°C/400°F/Gas 6.

2   Cut the skin from the pumpkin, remove the seeds and threads and cut the flesh into even-sized pieces. Cook in boiling water to cover until tender, then drain and mash with the butter.

3   Season with salt and pepper, and transfer half to a shallow gratin dish. Top with the goat's cheese, then spoon the rest of the pumpkin on top, sprinkle with the Parmesan cheese and bake for about 30 minutes, or until bubbling and golden brown.

12.0g carbs and 18.9g protein per serving

tarragon, almond and pecorino tart

PHASES

225g (8oz) almonds, finely ground
55g (2oz) butter
½ teaspoon salt

For the filling
2 eggs
2 egg yolks
300ml (½ pint) double cream
2 tablespoons chopped tarragon
100g (3½oz) Pecorino cheese, grated
freshly ground black pepper

Serves 6

PREPARATION 45 MINUTES • COOKING 45 MINUTES

This is a wonderful low-carb treat. It's extremely rich, but great for a special occasion. The pastry is made from almonds instead of flour but tastes very similar to normal shortcrust. It's best to use whole almonds and grind them yourself if possible, as including the brown skins raises the fibre content and thus lowers the carbs, as well as improving the flavour.

1 Preheat the oven to 180°C/350°F/Gas 4.

2 To make the pastry, mix the ground almonds, butter and salt together until it forms a dough – this can be done in a food processor.

3 Press the dough into a 20cm (8in) flan tin or dish. Prick the base of the flan all over and bake in the oven for 15 minutes, or until set and golden brown.

4 To make the filling, whisk together the eggs and egg yolks, and then gradually whisk in the cream. Add pepper (you will probably not need any salt as the cheese is quite salty).

5 Scatter the tarragon and grated cheese evenly over the flan then pour in the cream mixture. Bake for 25–30 minutes, or until golden brown and just set. Serve warm or cold.

5.1g carbs and 21g protein per serving

divine cauliflower bake

PHASES

PREPARATION 15 MINUTES • **COOKING** 45 MINUTES

1 medium cauliflower, in
   even-sized florets
150ml (¼ pint) soured
   cream
225g (8oz) grated Cheddar
   cheese
4 spring onions, finely
   chopped
a few drops of Tabasco
   sauce
salt and freshly ground
   black pepper

Serves 4

When baked this way cauliflower really lives up to the name 'Divine', and it is very easy to do. Although it can be a main course in its own right, it also makes a good potato substitute, particularly filling the 'jacket potato with cheese' gap.

1 Preheat the oven to 180°C/350°F/Gas 4.

2 Cook the cauliflower in 5cm (2in) of boiling water until tender, about 7–10 minutes. Drain thoroughly.

3 Mash the cauliflower; it's nice with some texture, although you could make it more or less smooth according to your taste. Stir in the soured cream, half the cheese, the spring onions and Tabasco sauce. Season with salt and pepper to taste.

4 Put the mixture into a shallow casserole dish, top with the rest of the cheese, and bake for about 35 minutes, or until crisp and golden brown.

7.7g carbs and 14.8g protein per serving

baby squash with sage, cream and gruyère

PHASES ② ③

4 baby gem squash
2 garlic cloves, crushed
4 tablespoons double or
   soya cream
55g (2oz) Gruyère cheese,
   grated
4 fresh sage leaves,
   chopped
salt and freshly ground
   black pepper

Serves 4

PREPARATION 10 MINUTES • **COOKING** 35 MINUTES

These baby squash with their creamy filling flavoured with fresh sage make an easy and delectable first course or light meal.

1 Preheat the oven to 180°C/350°F/Gas 4.

2 Slice the tops off the baby squash and scoop out the seeds. Rub the insides with salt, pepper and garlic.

3 Stand the squash in a casserole, pour a spoonful of cream into each and divide the cheese and sage between them, pushing them into the cavities. Replace the squash tops.

4 Bake the squash until they are tender, about 30–35 minutes, but don't let them overcook and burst. Serve immediately.

13.4g carbs and 4g protein per serving

swiss chard quiche

PHASES

PREPARATION 45 MINUTES • **COOKING** 1 HOUR

225g (8oz) almonds, finely
  ground
55g (2oz) butter
½ teaspoon salt

For the filling
225g (8oz) Swiss chard
28g (1oz) butter
200ml (7 fl oz) double or
  soya cream
3 egg yolks
freshly grated nutmeg
salt and freshly ground
  black pepper

Serves 6

Here is a low-carb version of a classic French tart. If you can't
get Swiss chard, you could use spinach instead.

1 Preheat the oven to 200°C/400°F/Gas 6. To make the pastry,
mix the ground almonds, butter and salt together until they
form a dough – this can be done in a food processor.

2 Press the dough into a 20cm (8in) flan tin. Prick the base very
lightly with a fork and bake for 15 minutes, or until the pastry
is crisp. Remove from the oven and turn the heat down to
160°C/325°F/Gas 3.

3 Meanwhile, make the filling. Wash the Swiss chard, separate
the stalks from the leaves, and chop both. Melt the butter in
a saucepan, and put in the stalks. Cover and cook for about
4 minutes, or until they are almost tender. Add the leaves,
cover and cook for a further 2–3 minutes, or until everything
is tender.

4 Remove from the heat and mix in the cream. Add the egg
yolks, and nutmeg, salt and pepper to taste, stirring well.
Pour the mixture into the flan case and bake for 25–30
minutes, or until the filling is set. Serve hot, warm or cold.

5.0g carbs and 13.4g protein per serving

shepherd's pie

PHASES ② ③

PREPARATION 20 MINUTES • **COOKING** 40 MINUTES

1 tablespoon olive oil
1 small onion, sliced
1 small green pepper,
  chopped
1 × 450g (1lb) packet frozen
  vegetarian 'mince'
1 × 400g (14oz) can
  chopped tomatoes in
  juice
1 garlic clove, crushed
1 tablespoon tomato purée
¼–½ teaspoon smoked
  paprika (optional)
1 teaspoon vegetable
  bouillon stock powder
6 tablespoons water
a little butter or vegan
  margarine or 55–115g
  (2–4oz) grated Cheddar
  or vegan cheese, to
  finish
salt and freshly ground
  black pepper

The smoked paprika gives this traditional dish a delicious, subtle flavour but you can omit it if you can't get hold of any. The filling is made with vegetarian 'mince', which you can find in the freezer section of any large supermarket, and the topping is a lovely cauliflower mash.

1 Preheat the oven to 200°C/400°F/Gas 6.

2 Heat the oil in a large frying pan, put in the onion and pepper, and cook for 5 minutes. Add the vegetarian 'mince' and cook for a further 2–3 minutes. Add the tomatoes, garlic, tomato purée, smoked paprika, if using, bouillon powder and water. Season to taste.

3 To make the cauliflower mash, cook the cauliflower florets in 5cm (2in) of boiling water for 5–7 minutes, or until tender. Drain well then transfer to a food processor with the butter or olive oil, soya milk or cream and some salt and pepper. Whizz until thick and smooth, like mashed potatoes.

4 Spoon the mince mixture into a shallow casserole and spread the cauliflower mash on top. Mark the surface with

For the cauliflower 'mash' topping

1 large 600g (1lb 5oz) cauliflower, broken into florets

28g (1oz) butter or 2 tablespoons olive oil

2–3 tablespoons soya milk or cream

Serves 4

the prongs of a fork and dot with butter or vegan margarine, or sprinkle generously with grated Cheddar or vegan cheese.

5 Bake for about 25 minutes, or until golden brown on top.

15g carbs and 31.3g protein per serving (but count extra carbs if using grated vegan cheese on top, as the different brands vary)

side vegetables

YOU CAN EAT MANY vegetables freely when you're low-carbing, especially once you are past the first stage of the diet, so what to serve 'on the side' isn't difficult. The vegetable many people miss is, of course, the potato, but there are some good low-carb replacements. Turnips, cauliflower and kohlrabi are all low in carbs and make flavoursome and useful potato replacements. For a mashed potato taste-alike, try the Hot Kohlrabi Mash or the cauliflower mash, which is given as a topping for the Shepherd's Pie on pages 120–1. What these versions lack in starchiness they gain in creamy butteriness – and that's a reason, too, for making the Turnip Gratin Dauphinoise, which, by low-carb standards, you can indulge in fairly guiltlessly... but not too often!

I included a recipe for a chip replacement in *The Vegetarian Low-Carb Diet* (using turnips instead of potatoes, cut into chip shapes and roasted in the oven). You can also roast cauliflower in the same way, and I think this makes one of the best chip/roast potato replacements because if you cook it long enough it becomes quite crisp around the edges. These vegetables are both so good that I've added a recipe for Roasted Vegetables in this chapter that uses both turnips and cauliflower.

Apart from that, there are several of my favourite vegetable dishes: Braised Celery that is so tender it melts in your mouth, and it is wonderfully low in carbs, Roasted Red Peppers Stuffed with Fennel, and one you can indulge in occasionally without guilt when you are low-carbing – Asparagus with Hollandaise Sauce.

braised celery

PHASES

PREPARATION 10 MINUTES • **COOKING** 1 HOUR 5 MINUTES

2 tablespoons of olive oil

2 celery hearts, trimmed
   and quartered

1 teaspoon crushed
   coriander seeds

1 bay leaf

6 peppercorns

600ml (1 pint) water

salt

chopped fresh parsley,
   to garnish

Serves 2

Cooked slowly, celery is meltingly delicious and a very useful
low-carb accompaniment to main dishes.

1 Put the olive oil in a large saucepan and fry the celery with
   the coriander seeds, bay leaf and peppercorns for 2–3
   minutes, then add a sprinkling of salt and the water.

2 Bring to the boil then reduce the heat, cover and leave to
   cook gently for about 1 hour, or until the celery is very tender.

3 Remove the celery with a slotted spoon, put it into a shallow
   dish and keep it warm.

4 Boil the remaining liquid hard to reduce it well, and pour
   it over the celery. Sprinkle with some chopped parsley
   and serve.

3g carbs and 1.4g protein per serving

hot kohlrabi mash on a bed of watercress

PHASES

700g (1lb 9oz) Kohlrabi,
   peeled and cut into
   even-sized pieces
15g (½oz) butter
2–3 tablespoons double
   or soya cream
1 bunch or packet of
   watercress
1 tablespoon walnut oil
a few drops of red wine
   vinegar
55g (2oz) walnuts,
   chopped
salt and freshly ground
   black pepper

Serves 4

PREPARATION 15 MINUTES • **COOKING** 10 MINUTES

Kohlrabi looks like some strange space-age vegetable, but it has a delicious, delicate flavour and one of the lowest carb counts of any root vegetable. Here it makes a lovely creamy mash, served with bright, contrasting watercress.

1 Cook the kohlrabi in boiling water to cover until tender, about 10 minutes. Drain and mash with the butter, cream, and salt and pepper to taste.

2 Toss the watercress with the walnut oil, vinegar and some salt and pepper.

3 To serve, divide the watercress among four plates, put a mound of the kohlrabi on top and sprinkle with the walnuts.

6.0g carbs and 5.4g protein per serving

vegan variation
Use soya cream and a tablespoonful of olive oil or vegan margarine instead of butter.

asparagus with hollandaise sauce

PHASES

PREPARATION 10 MINUTES • COOKING 10 MINUTES

450g (1lb) asparagus,
  trimmed
125g (4½oz) butter, diced
1 tablespoon lemon juice
2 egg yolks
sea salt
ground white pepper

Serves 2–4

Fresh young asparagus spears served with a traditional sauce – one of the best treats of summer, and it's low-carb!

1 Cook the asparagus in boiling water until tender, about 5 minutes or so, depending on the thickness and how crunchy you like it. Drain.

2 Meanwhile, make the sauce: melt the butter and bring to the boil. Whizz the lemon juice and egg yolks in a food processor or blender until pale and thick, then, with the machine still running, pour in the boiling melted butter and whizz for a further minute. Season with salt and a pinch of white pepper, and serve with the asparagus.

> **4.8g carbs and 8.7g protein per serving (if serving 2)**
> **2.4g carbs and 4.3g protein per serving (if serving 4)**

fennel à la grecque

PHASES ❷ ❸

4 fennel bulbs
2 tablespoons olive oil
1 tablespoon coriander
   seeds, crushed
4 strips of lemon peel
1 × 400g (14oz) can
   chopped tomatoes
salt and freshly ground
   black pepper

Serves 4

PREPARATION 10 MINUTES • **COOKING** 25 MINUTES

An aromatic tomato sauce complements fennel well, and this dish makes a pleasant starter or accompanying vegetable served hot, warm or cold.

1 Trim the fennel, saving any leafy sections. Pare off any chunky root parts, and if the outer leaves look tough, either remove them or pare them slightly with a sharp knife, depending on how edible they look. Cut the fennel down through the root into eighths.

2 Heat the oil in a heavy-based saucepan and put in the fennel. Turn the fennel so that it all becomes coated with the oil, then cover the pan and leave it to cook gently for 2–3 minutes. Add the coriander seeds, lemon peel and tomatoes. Cover and cook gently for 15–20 minutes, or until the fennel is very tender.

3 Remove from the heat, season with salt and pepper, and leave to cool. Add the reserved fennel leaves, chopped, just before serving.

12.9g carbs and 6.0g protein per serving

turnip gratin dauphinoise

PHASES

28g (1oz) butter
1 garlic clove, crushed
450g (1lb) turnips
freshly grated nutmeg
150ml (¼ pint) double
    cream
150ml (¼ pint) water
salt and freshly ground
    black pepper

Serves 4 (as a side dish)

PREPARATION 10 MINUTES • **COOKING** 1 HOUR

Meltingly soft turnip flavoured with a buttery garlic cream sauce makes a rich accompaniment to simple main dishes, and is truly mouth-watering.

1 Preheat the oven to 200°C/400°F/Gas 6.

2 Mix the butter with the crushed garlic and use half to grease a shallow casserole.

3 Peel the turnips and cut into very thin slices. Season with salt, pepper and nutmeg.

4 Layer the slices into the casserole. Pour the cream and the water over the top and dot with the remaining garlic butter. Cover with foil and bake for 1 hour, removing the foil about 20 minutes before the end of the cooking time.

6.7g carbs and 1.8g protein per serving

vegan variation

Use vegan margarine instead of butter and replace the double cream and water with 1 carton soya cream and 100ml (3½ fl oz) water.

roasted red peppers stuffed with fennel ⓥ

PHASES ② ③

2 small fennel bulbs
4 red peppers
1 × 400g (14oz) can
   tomatoes in juice
1 tablespoon coriander
   seeds, crushed
8 teaspoons olive oil
salt and freshly ground
   black pepper

Serves 4

PREPARATION 20 MINUTES • **COOKING** 1 HOUR 10 MINUTES

This is a way of cooking peppers which I like very much. It can be served hot or cold as a first course or accompanying vegetable. The red peppers need to be good medium-sized ones, rather square in shape; and the fennel bulbs need to be fairly small so that when cut into eighths two pieces will fit inside the peppers side by side.

1 Preheat the oven to 180°C/350°F/Gas 4.

2 Bring 2.5cm (1in) of water to the boil in a medium saucepan. Cut the leafy tops off the fennel and trim the root ends. Remove a layer of the white part if it looks as if it is tough. Cut the fennel down through the root end into quarters, then eighths, keeping them joined at the base. Cook the fennel in the water, covered, for 5–7 minutes, or until tender, then drain.

3 Halve the peppers, cutting right down through the stalks. Remove the seeds and trim the white part inside to make a good cavity. Arrange the peppers in a roasting tin or shallow casserole dish.

4 Chop the tomatoes and divide the mixture between the peppers, adding a little of the juice as necessary. Season with salt and freshly ground black pepper, then place two pieces of fennel side by side inside the peppers and on top of the tomato, with the root-end towards the stem end of

the pepper. Push them down neatly to fit, and season again. Sprinkle with the coriander seeds and pour 1 teaspoonful of olive oil over the top of each pepper half. Bake, uncovered, for about 1 hour, or until very tender and beginning to brown. Serve hot or cold.

15.1g carbs and 4.5g protein per serving

roasted vegetables

PHASES

PREPARATION 15 MINUTES • **COOKING** 45–60 MINUTES

1 cauliflower, in florets
450g (1lb) turnips, in even-sized pieces
4 tablespoons olive oil
rind and juice of 1 lemon

Serves 4

When we think of roasted vegetables we often choose potatoes, but other vegetables roast extremely well. Cauliflower and turnip are used here tossed in olive oil and lemon juice, which really brings out their flavour.

1 Preheat the oven to 200°C/400°F/Gas 6.

2 Put the vegetables onto a roasting tin and toss with the oil and lemon juice.

3 Put into the oven and cook for 45–60 minutes, or until tender and browned in places.

12.6g carbs and 4.8g protein per serving

hot and cold desserts

MAKING GOOD DESSERTS is one of the challenges of low-carb cooking, but there are some useful ingredients that make them possible: rhubarb and berries are low enough in carbs to be enjoyed quite freely once you're past the first stage; peaches and plums can also be used, and many low-carbers can also get away with apples, pears and oranges in the later stages, although I haven't used these in the recipes here. Cream – both double and soya – is fine to use, and ground almonds make a fantastic flour replacement; just try the Rhubarb Pie, Plum Crumble and Strawberry Cheesecake to test this out.

Included are various custards and creams, a compôte and a stunning Lemon and Vodka Sorbet. You will also find a Chocolate and Raspberry Layer that uses a fantastic cocoa and coconut-oil chocolate mixture, which sets hard and crisp, to make one of the most indulgent (yet surprisingly healthy) puddings you could wish for.

There is more information on all the key ingredients, including coconut oil, and also notes on the various sweeteners that can be used in low-carb cooking, on pages 18–21.

vodka and lemon sorbet

PHASES

125ml (4 fl oz) water
100g (3½oz) xylitol or your
    chosen low-carb
    sweetener, see recipe
    introduction
grated rind of 1 lemon
125ml (4 fl oz) freshly
    squeezed lemon juice
    (juice of about 3 lemons)
2 tablespoons vodka
strands of lemon rind or
    mint sprigs, to decorate

Serves 4

PREPARATION 10 MINUTES PLUS AT LEAST 5 HOURS FREEZING
COOKING 5 MINUTES

I use xylitol (see page 19) to sweeten this fabulous sorbet
because the slightly aniseed flavour of stevia, my normal
preferred low-carb sweetener, seems to come through too
much in this particular recipe. If you are happy with an
artificial sweetener such as Splenda you could use that, or
have a try with stevia and see what you think. The version as
given is wonderful, and, because of the vodka, it never gets
too solid so it can be served straight from the freezer.

1 Put the water into a saucepan with the xylitol and heat
   gently to dissolve. Remove from the heat and cool.

2 Stir the lemon rind and juice into the cooled mixture, and
   add the vodka. Pour into a suitable container for freezing
   and freeze until crystals form. (This will take several hours
   because the alcohol in the vodka slows up the process.) Break
   up the crystals using a fork or an electric beater and return
   the sorbet to the freezer. Freeze until firm.

3 Scrape the mixture into glasses and serve, decorated with
   some strands of lemon rind or mint sprigs.

3.2g carbs and 0.2g protein per serving

raspberry and rose layer

PHASES

300ml (½ pint) plain
   Greek yogurt
300ml (½ pint) double
   cream
2–3 teaspoons rose water
stevia or your chosen low-
   carb sweetener, to taste
350g (12oz) raspberries
rose petals, to decorate

Serves 6

PREPARATION 10 MINUTES, PLUS CHILLING TIME

Rose water makes a luxuriously flavoured cream for this raspberry dessert. It's a little like a trifle, without the sponge cake or jelly!

1 Put the yogurt and cream into a bowl and whisk together until thick. Add the rose water and stevia or sweetener to taste.

2 Sprinkle the raspberries with stevia or sweetener as necessary.

3 Spoon layers of raspberries and the rose cream into six deep glasses, starting with the raspberries, then cream, followed by more raspberries, and a final layer of cream. Cover and chill until needed. Scatter some pink rose petals on top before serving.

6.8g carbs and 3.3g protein per serving

fruit and flower compôte in rosehip tea

PHASES ② ③

6 rosehip, hibiscus and
 raspberry tea bags
225ml (8 fl oz) boiling
 water
4 ripe peaches
200g (7oz) fresh
 raspberries
stevia or your chosen low-
 carb sweetener, to taste
rose petals and a few
 small summer flowers
 such as borage, lavender
 and pinks, to decorate

Serves 4

PREPARATION 10 MINUTES, PLUS AT LEAST 1 HOUR
STEEPING TIME

This compôte is slightly higher in carbs than many of the
pudding recipes in this book, but perfectly allowable if you
plan for it in the later stages of the diet, or in maintenance –
and you can have it with cream if you like! The tea gives
this compôte an intriguing flavour. Look for tea bags that
contain rosehip, hibiscus and/or raspberry. There are plenty
to choose from.

1 Put the teabags into a bowl with 225ml (8 fl oz) boiling water.

2 Cut the peaches into thin slices, discarding the stones. Add
   the slices to the bowl with the raspberries and mix gently.
   Add stevia or artificial sweetener to taste. Cover and leave
   for at least an hour for all the flavours to develop.

3 Just before serving the fruit salad, remove the teabags,
   squeezing as much liquid as possible into the salad. Serve
   the compôte in a shallow glass bowl with the petals and
   flowers scattered on top.

14.1g carbs and 1.9g protein per serving

blackberry fool

PHASES

400g (14oz) blackberries
150ml (¼ pint) double
    cream
150ml (¼ pint) plain Greek
    yogurt
stevia or your chosen low-
    carb sweetener, to taste

Serves 4

PREPARATION 10 MINUTES • **COOKING** 10 MINUTES

If you are in the countryside in late summer when the newly ripening blackberries are sun-kissed and at their sweetest, this is the best time to make this heavenly fool. The sweeter the blackberries are the better, because you'll need to add less stevia or sweetener.

1   Wash the blackberries, then put them into a saucepan with only the water that clings to them. Cook over a gentle heat for a few minutes, or until the juices run and the blackberries are very tender – watch them carefully and add a few drops of water if they start to catch in the pan. Cool.

2   Whisk the cream until standing in soft peaks then add the yogurt and blackberries, stirring gently. Taste and add a little stevia or sweetener, if necessary.

3   Divide between four bowls and serve at once, or chill.

7g carbs and 3.4g protein per serving

plum crumble

PREPARATION 15 MINUTES • COOKING 35 MINUTES

500g (1lb 2oz) red plums, halved and stones removed
2–3 tablespoons water
stevia or your chosen low-carb sweetener, to taste
175g (6oz) ground almonds
85g (3oz) butter
a pinch of ground cinnamon
double or soya cream (optional)

Serves 4–6

Once you are past the first stage of the low-carb diet, plums are not too high in carbs to enjoy and can be made into a lovely crumble. It's gorgeous served hot with lashings of cream.

1 Preheat the oven to 180°C/350°F/Gas 4.

2 Cook the plums in 2–3 tablespoons of water in a covered pan for about 15 minutes, or until tender. Remove from the heat and sweeten to taste with stevia or your choice of low-carb sweetener. Cool.

3 Put the ground almonds, butter and cinnamon into a bowl. Mix with a fork or your fingers to a crumbly consistency. Add a little stevia or sweetener to taste, then spoon the crumble on top of the plums.

4 Bake for about 20 minutes, or until crisp and golden. Serve at once with cream, if you like.

16.1g carbs and 13.1g protein per serving (if serving 4); 10.7g carbs and 8.7g protein (if serving 6); if adding cream, count the carbs

vegan variation
Replace the butter with vegan margarine and serve with soya cream instead of double cream.

strawberry cheesecake

PHASES

100g (3½oz) ground
    almonds
15g (½oz) butter, softened
850g (1lb 14oz) cream
    cheese
4 eggs
300ml (½ pint) double
    cream
grated rind of 2 lemons
stevia or your chosen low-
    carb sweetener, to taste
1 × 142ml (5 fl oz) carton
    soured cream
100g (3½oz) strawberries

Serves 8

PREPARATION 15 MINUTES • **COOKING** 1 HOUR 15 MINUTES
(PLUS CHILLING TIME)

A luxurious pudding, which looks and tastes wonderful.
I really love this cheesecake with its delicious almond base;
it's excellent and very much like a traditional one.

1   Preheat the oven to 220°C/425°F/Gas 7.

2   Mix the almonds and butter together to make a dough –
    this can be done in a food processor. Press into the base of a
    20cm (8in) spring-release tin and bake for 10–15 minutes, or
    until set and crisp. Remove from the oven and reduce the
    heat to 180°C/350°F/Gas 4.

3   Beat the cream cheese until soft, then whisk in the eggs,
    double cream and lemon rind. Add stevia or sweetener to
    taste; I find 2 teaspoonfuls of pure stevia powder is right for
    this, but the types and strengths vary, so taste and check,
    remembering that baking will dull the flavour a little.

4   Pour the filling into the tin, on top of the crisp almond base.
    Then put the cheesecake in the oven and bake for 1 hour.
    Cover the top with foil towards the end if it's getting too
    brown. Then turn off the oven, open the door slightly and
    leave the cheesecake until cold, if possible.

5   Leave to chill in the refrigerator in the tin until required –
    overnight is best, if there is time.

6   To finish the cheesecake, remove from the tin and spread the

soured cream all over the top. Then slice the strawberries very thinly and arrange them on top of the soured cream. Chill until needed, but don't make this too far in advance – an hour or two is fine, as the strawberries lose their brightness if left for much longer.

6.6g carbs and 15.2g protein per serving

little coffee treats

PHASES

PREPARATION 10 MINUTES, PLUS TIME TO CHILL

225g (8oz) mascarpone

2 teaspoons good-quality strong instant coffee granules

tablespoon almost boiling water

stevia or your chosen low-carb sweetener, to taste

Serves 2

It takes no time at all to prepare these very rich and delicious little treats made with creamy, soft mascarpone. Use good-quality instant coffee for the best flavour.

1 Put the mascarpone into a bowl and stir a little to make it smooth. Put the coffee granules into a cup and add about a tablespoonful of almost-boiling water – just enough to dissolve them. Add the coffee to the bowl and stir until it's all well combined.

2 Sweeten to taste with stevia or artificial sweetener of your choice.

3 Spoon into two bowls, and chill until ready to serve.

2.6g carbs and 2.4g protein per serving

rhubarb pie

PHASES

225g (8oz) ground
   almonds
55g (2oz) butter, softened
1 teaspoon baking powder

For the filling
500g (1lb 2oz) rhubarb cut
   into 2.5cm (1in) pieces
grated rind of 1 orange
2–3 tablespoons water
stevia or your chosen low-
   carb sweetener, to taste

Serves 8

PREPARATION 15 MINUTES • **COOKING** 30 MINUTES

Very low in carbs, rhubarb can be made into an excellent low-carb traditional top-crust pie. It also works well with canned unsweetened rhubarb, if you find this more convenient – see Spiced Rhubarb Compôte on page 139.

1   Preheat the oven to 180°C/350°F/Gas 4.

2   To make the filling, put the rhubarb into a saucepan with the orange rind and 2–3 tablespoons of water. Cover and cook gently for a few minutes, or until tender. Remove from the heat and sweeten to taste with stevia or your choice of low-carb sweetener. Cool and transfer to a pie dish.

3   Mix the ground almonds, butter and baking powder together to make a dough – this can be done in a food processor.

4   Moisten the edges of the pie dish with water. Form the dough roughly into a shape that is the same as your pie dish (round, oval, rectangular or square). Put the dough between two sheets of baking parchment and roll out to fit your pie dish. Peel off the top piece of paper and invert the rolled dough over the dish. Press the dough into the dish, through the paper, then peel off the paper. Neaten the pastry with your fingers, pressing in any stray edges. There's no need to trim off any pastry, as it is so soft you can simply press it into place. Make a steam hole or two in the centre.

5   Bake for about 25 minutes, or until the pastry is set, crisp and golden-brown. Serve hot, warm or cold.

vegan variation

Use vegan margarine instead of butter.

spiced rhubarb compôte

PHASES

PREPARATION 10 MINUTES • **COOKING** 5–10 MINUTES

900g (2lb) rhubarb
8 cloves
good pinch of ground
   ginger
stevia or your chosen low-
   carb sweetener, to taste

Serves 4–6

Rhubarb is a gift for low-carbers because it's almost carb-free. You can buy cans of unsweetened rhubarb and these are useful for making quick puddings, sweetening them to taste, as required, with stevia or an artificial sweetener. Fresh rhubarb is even better and in this compôte the warming spices add to the sweetness.

1 Trim the rhubarb and strip off any stringy parts then cut into 2.5cm (1in) lengths. Put into a heavy-based saucepan with the cloves and ginger.

2 Cover and cook over a gentle heat for about 5 minutes, or until soft.

3 Sweeten to taste with stevia or your choice of artificial sweetener. Transfer the rhubarb to a bowl, removing the cloves as you do so. Cover and chill.

chocolate and raspberry layer

PHASES

115g (4oz) almonds
150g (5½oz) virgin coconut
    oil
4 teaspoons cocoa powder
stevia or your chosen low-
    carb sweetener, to taste
150ml (¼ pint) double
    cream
100g (3½oz) raspberries

Serves 6

PREPARATION 20 MINUTES • **COOKING** 3–4 MINUTES

This recipe uses the Chocolate Almond Bark recipe from *The Vegetarian Low-Carb Diet,* and dresses it up for a party! You make the chocolate mixture in two round sandwich tins then turn the resulting two thin chocolate discs out, sandwich them together with raspberries and cream, and serve it in wedges, like cake. (For more about coconut oil, see page 18.)

1　Line the base of two 15cm (6in) round sandwich tins with circles of baking parchment. If you also line the sides with a small strip it will make the discs easier to get out. Then place the tins in the freezer to chill while you prepare the mixture.

2　Put the almonds in a coffee grinder and grind them fairly finely but not to a powder. Spread them out on a baking tin or grill pan and toast under a hot grill for 1–2 minutes, or until golden-brown.

3　Meanwhile, melt the coconut oil in a saucepan over a gentle heat, taking care not to let it get too hot.

4　Remove from the heat and stir in the cocoa powder, toasted almonds and stevia or sweetener to taste.

5　Pour the mixture straight into the chilled and lined tins, dividing it equally between them and making sure it covers the base of the tins evenly. Transfer to the freezer for 15–20 minutes, or until it has set hard.

6 Carefully ease the circles out of the tins and strip off the paper. Keep the circles in the freezer until you are ready to assemble them.

7 Whip the double cream and lightly mix with the raspberries. Spread all over one of the discs. Place the other disc on top and press down to make a sandwich. Keep cold until required, then cut, like a cake, with a sharp knife.

3.4g carbs and 4.9g protein per serving

lemon grass custards

PHASES ❶ ❷ ❸

3 lemon grass stalks,
    crushed
300ml (½ pint) double
    cream
2 eggs and 2 egg yolks
stevia or your chosen low-
    carb sweetener, to taste
herb flowers, such as sage,
    to decorate

Serves 4

PREPARATION 15 MINUTES, PLUS 15 MINUTES TO INFUSE
COOKING 55 MINUTES

The lemon grass gives these little creams a delicate and delectable fragrance and flavour, and they look very pretty decorated with herb flowers.

1 Preheat the oven to 160°C/325°F/Gas 3.

2 Put the lemon grass into a saucepan with the cream and bring to the boil, then cover and leave for 15 minutes for the flavour to infuse.

3 Meanwhile, whisk the eggs and egg yolks until frothy but not thick. Remove the lemon grass from the cream and bring back to the boil, then pour over the egg mixture.

4 Taste and sweeten with stevia or artificial sweetener as necessary. Strain into four individual ramekins and put them into a roasting tin. Cover with foil, pour boiling water into the roasting tin to come two-thirds up the sides of the ramekins, and bake for about 40–45 minutes, or until the custards are set.

5 Remove them from the oven, take them out of the tin and leave to cool. Decorate with herb flowers before serving.

2.2g carbs and 5.8g protein per serving

bread and baked treats

THIS SECTION STARTS with a low-carb baking mix, which works out much cheaper than any specialist ones you can buy, and works a treat. You can use it to replace the baking mix (or self-raising flour) specified in any low-carb recipes. Generally, though, I find ground almonds or soya – either soya flour or soya protein isolate powder (see page 150) – replace flour perfectly, with the addition of some baking powder if you want the mixture to rise.

Low-carb loaves are available in specialist shops and I have included several recipes for yeast and non-yeast versions in *The Vegetarian Low-Carb Diet*. The two 'breads' in this section are quick to make and useful as replacements for granary rolls and cornbread.

The Hazelnut Shortbread and Chocolate Bars are just for fun, and the Chocolate Cake is amazing – another of those low-carb recipes that uses 'normal' ingredients to produce something that anyone would enjoy (and not realise was low-carb unless you told them!).

baking mix

PHASES   **PREPARATION** 5 MINUTES

115g (4oz) soya flour
115g (4oz) non-GMO soya
   protein isolate powder
2 tablespoons baking
   powder
1 teaspoon salt
pinch of stevia or
   2 tablespoons of your
   chosen low-carb
   sweetener (optional)

Makes about 225g (8oz)

There are various low-carb alternatives to flour. You can simply use ground almonds for some recipes (see the pastry, crumble and cornbread recipes in this book, for example) or, for some recipes, you can use soya flour or soya protein isolate powder. However, if you are following a low-carb cake recipe you might like to use a low-carb baking mix. Although you can buy this, it's really easy (and much cheaper) to make your own. Here is the recipe.

Mix all the ingredients together and store in an airtight container.

28g carbs and 147g protein for the whole quantity
12g carbs and 65g protein per 100g (3½oz)

'cornbread'

PREPARATION 10 MINUTES • **COOKING** 20 MINUTES

55g (2oz) butter, melted
4 eggs
200g (7oz) ground
   almonds
1 teaspoon baking powder
a pinch of salt

Makes 16

Ground almonds form the base of this bread, which is very like cornbread with a solid, satisfying texture.

1 Preheat the oven to 180°C/350°F/Gas 4. Line a 20cm (8in) square tin with baking parchment.

2 Whisk together the butter and eggs, then gradually mix in the ground almonds, baking powder and a pinch of salt.

3 Tip the mixture into the prepared tin, level the top, and bake for 20 minutes, or until a skewer inserted into the centre comes out clean. Cool, then cut into 16 pieces to serve.

1.1g carbs and 5.1g protein per serving

hazelnut shortbread

PHASES

85g (3oz) hazelnuts,
  roasted and ground
25g (1oz) coconut oil,
  melted
stevia or your chosen low-
  carb sweetener

Makes about 6 slices

PREPARATION 15 MINUTES • **COOKING** 10 MINUTES PLUS
30–60 MINUTES FREEZING

This is an unusual, uncooked shortbread, which is set by the
coconut oil. Keep it in the refrigerator so that it stays crisp.
It makes an appealing tea-time treat and can also be topped
with strawberries and cream as a special pudding.

1 Line a plate or a small square tin with baking parchment.

2 Mix everything together adding stevia or low-carb
  sweetener to taste. Spread out on the plate or tin.

3 Freeze until firm. Use a sharp knife to cut into pieces.

1g carbs and 2.1g protein per slice

'granary' rolls

PHASES ② ③

PREPARATION 20 MINUTES • **COOKING** 40 MINUTES

3 eggs, separated
55g (2oz) cream cheese
1 tablespoon soya flour
1 tablespoon gluten
   powder
3 tablespoons wheat bran
2 tablespoons ground flax
1 teaspoon baking powder
2–3 tablespoons water

Makes 6

In truth, these look more like rather sunken soufflés than bread rolls, but they taste good and can be split and buttered or stuffed with filling. For a note about gluten powder, which is a useful ingredient in low-carb cooking, see page 17; if you can't get it, use plain wholemeal flour instead and increase the carbs by 1g per roll.

1 Preheat the oven to 230°C/450°F/Gas 8. Line a baking sheet with a piece of baking parchment.

2 Mix the egg yolks with the cream cheese, soya flour, gluten powder, wheat bran, ground flax, baking powder and water, to make a batter-like consistency.

3 Whisk the egg whites until stiff, then fold into the batter.

4 Divide the mixture into six portions. Form each into a roll and place on the baking sheet.

5 Put into the oven then immediately turn down the oven setting to 150°C/300°F/Gas 2 and bake for 20 minutes. Then reduce the setting again, to 140°C/275°F/Gas 1 and cook for a further 20 minutes, or until the rolls are brown and firm to the touch. Cool on a wire rack.

1.6g carbs and 5.7g protein per roll

chocolate cake

PHASES

PREPARATION 15 MINUTES • **COOKING** 35 MINUTES

85g (3oz) butter, softened
2 tablespoons olive oil
3 eggs
200g (7oz) ground
   almonds
1 tablespoon cocoa
   powder
1 teaspoon baking powder
1 teaspoon pure stevia or
   your chosen low-carb
   sweetener
1–2 tablespoons water

Makes about 6 slices

This is a lovely, moist, light-textured cake. You would never know it was low-carb and, if you use stevia, it's made with completely natural ingredients.

1 Preheat the oven to 160°C/325°F/Gas 3. Line a 15–18cm (6–7in) cake tin with baking parchment.

2 Whisk together the butter, olive oil and eggs until creamy. Stir in the ground almonds, cocoa powder, baking powder and the stevia or sweetener. Add the water to make a soft consistency that drops easily off the spoon.

3 Spoon the mixture into the tin and gently level the top. Bake for 30–35 minutes, or until risen and firm to a light touch, and a skewer inserted into the centre comes out clean.

4 Leave to cool on a wire rack, then strip off the paper.

> **18.5g carbs and 76.7g protein for the whole cake;
> 3.1g carbs and 12.8g protein per slice (if cutting into
> six slices)**

chocolate bars

PHASES

PREPARATION 15 MINUTES • **COOKING** 2–3 MINUTES

125g (4½oz) coconut oil

2 tablespoons (55g/2oz) crunchy peanut butter

1 teaspoon vanilla extract

2 scoops chocolate-flavoured soya protein isolate powder

1 scoop microfiltered whey powder (optional)

1½oz unsweetened desiccated coconut

Makes 16 bars

I feel I have to start this recipe with a warning: these are incredibly moreish and, although very low in carbs, they are high in calories so could sabotage any diet, low-carb or otherwise, unless eaten very sparingly. However, as an occasional treat, they really do hit the chocolate spot.

1 Line a shallow rectangular tin 16 × 25cm (6¼ × 10in) with baking parchment.

2 Put the coconut oil and peanut butter into a saucepan and melt over a gentle heat. Remove from the stove and stir in the vanilla, soya protein isolate powder, whey and coconut.

3 Pour the mixture into the tin, making sure it is even, then put into the freezer and chill completely – it needs to be really hard. Note that if you taste the mixture before it's frozen you may find the texture rather strange; however once frozen, it changes to *almost* that of chocolate.

4 Cut into 16 bars. Store in the freezer – they can be eaten straight from the freezer. (You could, of course, cut them into smaller pieces, like squares of fudge.)

12.4g carbs and 84.8g protein for the whole quantity; 0.8g carbs and 5.3g protein per bar

sources and stockists

ingredients and products

gluten powder

I'm hoping this will soon become available by the packet in health stores. You can, however, order it over the internet, as I do, from www.flourbin.com/index2.htm. The product is excellent and the company is helpful. However, you do have to make a minimum order of £10 and pay for carriage on top of that. The gluten powder keeps well; store it in the freezer, if necessary, or find some friends to share the order. For more information, the e-mail address is info@flourbin.com, tel: 01246 850124

soya protein isolate powder

Holland & Barrett stock a large 900g (2lb) tub of this, which I find great for baking and cooking. Holland & Barrett have assured me that it is GMO-free, although they do not state this on the label because all their products are in fact GMO-free. (They also stock a chocolate one, but it contains artificial sweeteners.)

My favourite soya protein isolate powder is Jarrow Formulas Iso-Rich Soy. It is very light and fine textured, unsweetened, with a delicate natural vanilla flavouring, guaranteed organic (which means there are no chemical residues from the processing) and great for making shakes. However, it is only available in a 450g (1lb) tub and is quite pricey because it has to be imported from the US. You can find out more about this, and order it by post if you wish, from Jan Freeman at Vitamin UK, PO Box 98, Manchester M20 6PZ, Freephone 0800 056 8148 (within the UK) or tel: 00 44 161 434 2876 (outside the UK). Jan is very helpful and can also advise you about vitamins and xylitol. The website is www.vitaminuk.com.

stevia

You can't buy this in the UK because it is illegal for anyone to sell it to you (see www.stevia.net/thesteviastory for more about this). It is, however, easy to buy from many websites and the ones I've dealt with have been friendly, helpful and efficient.

Try the Stevita Company for stevia with 'bulkers', which add about 1g carbs per serving, but which some people find is the easiest way to use stevia, and for liquid stevia, which some people like. Their address is 7650 US Hwy.287 #100, Arlington, Texas 76001, USA , tel +(1) 817 483 0044, fax +(1) 817 478 8891. The website is www.stevitastevia.com.

For pure stevia powder (and dried leaves, etc., if you want them), try www.emperorsherbologist.com/buy-stevioside.html. I have had some excellent pure stevia from them. I prefer the pure type without bulkers, but I suggest you start with really small amounts of different types and see which you like best.

I've also heard good things about www.nowfoods.com/?action=itemdetail&item_id=3143. Other sites you can try are: www.cookingwithstevia.com/stevia_faq.html and www.stepa.be/faqs.html. Also try www.herb-care.com/zmission.asp?_id=22, which tells you all about stevia and you can also buy it from there. There are several forms available, including jars of 'spoonable' stevia, which is carb-free and might be easier to measure out and use. It is probably worth trying this although I have not yet done so.

whey powder

I recommend you get a good-quality microfiltered type. I like Solgar Whey-to-Go in vanilla. (It is also available in chocolate, but this is higher in carbs.) It is not as easy to track down as I would like, but is available from top-quality health stores and you could also find the cheapest source on the internet; it is available from many suppliers. If you like it, the large size works out a lot cheaper. For stockists, contact Solgar Vitamin & Herb Ltd, Aldbury, Tring HP23 5PT, tel: 01442 890355 fax: 01442 890366.

xylitol

Not widely available in the UK at the time of writing but probably obtainable over the Internet. I buy it through Jan Freeman of Vitamin UK, see above.

books

Rose Elliot, *The Vegetarian Low-Carb Diet*, Piatkus, 2005 (full details on how to do the vegetarian low-carb diet, menu plans for the first fortnight, recipes and a useful carb and protein counter).

Corinne T. Netzer, *The Complete Book of Food Counts*, CTN, 2003 (for more about carb counts).

useful websites

My own website gives information about my books and the vegetarian and vegan lifestyle. It also includes recipes and tips: www.roseelliot.com

A very useful US site that allows you to find nutritional information, including carb and protein counts for many foods: www.nalusda.gov/fnic/foodscomp/search/

For information on coconut oil: www.coconut-info.com

For facts about artificial sweeteners: www.holisticmed.com/splenda/

For facts about the safety of soya: www.foodrevolution.org/what_about_soy_htm, and www.veganoutreach.org/health/soysafe.html

For facts about stevia: www.cookingwithstevia.com/ and www.cookingwithstevia.com/stevia_faq.html

For a very friendly, helpful vegetarian low-carb forum you can join to exchange information and experiences, and ask questions: www.immuneweb.org/lists/lcweb.html and click on 'LCVeg'.

index

Aioli, Baby Vegetables with 56–7
almonds 116, 145
artichoke hearts 52
asparagus 102
    Asparagus Frittata 33
    Asparagus with Hollandaise Sauce 125
    Quick Asparagus, Quorn and Red
        Pepper Stir-fry 99
aspartame 18
Avocado, Chunky, and Coriander Dip 76

Baby Squash with Sage, Cream and
    Gruyère 118
Baby Vegetables with Aioli 56–7
bad breath 7
baked treats 143–9
Baking Mix 143, 144
baking parchment 13
barbecues 80, 86
Bitterleaf Salad with Walnut
    Dressing 46
Blackberry Fool 134
blenders 13
Blue Cheese Dip 74–5
Blueberries, Orange Waffles with 34–5
bones, healthy 5
breads 143–9
breakfasts 29–37
Broccoli and Brie Bake 111
butter 17

cabbage 102
    Cabbage Cannelloni 106–7
    Cabbage, Mushroom and Peanut
        Stir-fry 100
    Cabbage Tagliatelle with Cream
        Cheese and Mushroom Sauce 103
    Warm Red Cabbage and Cherry
        Tomato Salad 53
Cake, Chocolate 148
Camembert, Deep-fried 91
Carb Cleanse (Phase 1) 6, 7, 9
carbohydrates 4–5
    counting 7–10, 11
cauliflower 56–7
    Divine Cauliflower Bake 117

Green Peppers Stuffed with
    Cauliflower Cheese 89
celery
    Braised Celery 123
    Celery and Tomato Salsa 53
    Cream of Celery Soup 42
cereals 30–1
cheese 14
cheese dishes
    Baby Squash with Sage, Cream and
        Gruyère 118
    Blue Cheese Dip 74–5
    Broccoli and Brie Bake 111
    Cabbage Tagliatelle with Cream
        Cheese and Mushroom Sauce 103
    Cheese Crackers 79
    Courgettes Parmesan 110
    Deep-fried Camembert 91
    Divine Cauliflower Bake 117
    Goat's Cheese Dip 73
    Green Peppers Stuffed with
        Cauliflower Cheese 89
    Grilled Courgette with Halloumi
        Cheese 85
    Little Coffee Treats 136–7
    Mockeroni Cheese 108
    Pumpkin and Goat's Cheese
        Gratin 115
    Quick Creamy Cheese Sauce 59, 60
    Salad Roulade 50–1
    Spaghetti Squash with Dolcelatte
        Cream and Walnuts 104
    Spinach Roulade with Mozzarella
        and Tomato Filling 112–13
    Strawberry Cheesecake 136–7
    Tarragon, Almond and Pecorino
        Tart 116
    Watercress and Red Pepper with
        Mascarpone 54–5
Cheesecake, Strawberry 136–7
chicory 46
    Chicory, Red Leaf and Watercress
        Salad 49
chips 77–8
Chocolate Bars 149
Chocolate Cake 148

Chocolate and Raspberry Layer 140–1
cholesterol 6
cinnamon
    Cream of Swede Soup with
        Cinnamon 39
    Hot Cinnamon Cereal 30
coconut oil 18
coffee, Little Coffee Treats 137
coffee grinders, electric 13
cold-pressed vegetable oils 18
compôtes
    Fruit and Flower Compôte in
        Rosehip Tea 133
    Spiced Rhubarb Compôte 139
Continued Weightloss (Phase 2) 6, 9
coriander 53
    Chunky Avocado and Coriander
        Dip 76
    Vegetable Curry with Coriander
        Raita 94–5
'Cornbread' 145
Coulis, Raspberry 69
courgettes 56–7, 102
    Courgette Chips 77
    Courgettes Parmesan 110
    Grilled Courgette with Halloumi
        Cheese 85
    Stuffed Courgettes with Fresh
        Tomato Sauce 90
Crackers, Cheese 79
cream 17
Cream of Celery Soup 42
Cream of Swede Soup with
    Cinnamon 39
Cream of Watercress Soup 44
Creamy Tomato Sauce 67
'Crisps', Daikon 75
croutons 38
Crumble, Plum 135
cucumber, Piquant Cucumber Salad 48
Custards, Lemon Grass 142

Daikon 'Crisps' 75
desserts 130–42
dips and dippers 70–9
dressings 59–69

drinks 12, 22–8

eggs 14
egg dishes
    Asparagus Frittata 33
    Lemon Grass Custards 142
    Lightly Curried Eggs 36
    Omelette Cannelloni with Spinach
        Filling 105
Eggless Mayo 59, 61

fat stores 4
fats and oils 6, 12, 15, 17–18
fennel 56–7
    Fennel à la Grecque 126
    Fennel, Tomato and Black Olive
        Salad 55
    Grilled Fennel with Radicchio and
        Garlic Cream 86–7
    Roasted Red Peppers Stuffed with
        Fennel 128–9
Fettuccini of Summer Vegetables 102
flax seed oil 18
flax seeds 15
flour substitute 143, 144
Fool, Blackberry 134
Frapuccino, Fabulous 26
Fresh Herbal Dip 74
fridges 14
Frittata, Asparagus 33
fruit 9–10, 21
Fruit and Flower Compôte in Rosehip
    Tea 133

garlic 86–7
gluten powder 17, 150
glycogen 5
Goat's Cheese Dip 73
Gomasio, Japanese-style Salad with
    Dipping Sauce and 58
Goulash 93
'Granary' Rolls 147
Granola, Low Carb 31
Gravy, Rich Mushroom 65
Green Peppers Stuffed with Cauliflower
    Cheese 89
Green Salad with Toasted Hazelnuts 52

hazelnuts
    Green Salad with Toasted
        Hazelnuts 52

Hazelnut Shortbread 146
Hollandaise Sauce, Asparagus with 125

insulin 3, 5, 6

Japanese-style Salad with Dipping Sauce
    and Gomasio 58

ketosis 7
kidney damage 5
kitchen equipment 13–14
kohlrabi
    Hot Kohlrabi Mash on a Bed of
        Watercress 124
    Kohlrabi and Radish Salad 57

lemon
    Lemon Cheesecake Smoothie 25
    Ricotta and Lemon Pancakes 32
    Vodka and Lemon Sorbet 131
Lemon Grass Custards 142
Lettuce Salad Wraps 47

main meals
    bakes 109–21
    curries, casseroles and stir-fries
        92–100
    fried, braised and grilled 80–91
Maintenance (Phase 3) 6, 9
maltitol 19
Mash, Hot Kohlrabi, on a Bed of
    Watercress 124
mayonnaise 18
    Eggless Mayo 59, 61
Melon and Mint Cooler 24
mince, vegetarian 16, 92, 120–1
mushrooms
    Cabbage, Mushroom and Peanut
        Stir-fry 100
    Cabbage Tagliatelle with Cream
        Cheese and Mushroom Sauce 103
    Layered Oyster Mushroom Loaf
        114–15
    Mushroom 'Caviar' 71
    Porcini Sauce 66
    Ragoût of Wild Mushrooms 97
    Rich Mushroom Gravy 65
    Wild Mushroom Dip 72
mustard 48
net carbs 8
Nettle Soup 43

nut butters 15
nuts 15, 22, 46, 52, 100, 104, 146

Okra, Baby Sweetcorn and Spiced
    Pumpkin Casserole 96
olive oil 18, 59
Olives, Black, Fennel and Tomato
    Salad 55
omega-3 fatty acids 15, 18
Omelette Cannelloni with Spinach
    Filling 105
onions 58
Orange Waffles with Blueberries 34–5

pancakes
    'Potato' Pancakes 35
    Ricotta and Lemon Pancakes 32
paprika 40
'pasta' dishes 101–8
peaches 133
Peanut, Cabbage and Mushroom
    Stir-fry 100
Peppermint Tea 28
peppers
    Green Peppers Stuffed with
        Cauliflower Cheese 89
    Quick Asparagus, Quorn and Red
        Pepper Stir-fry 99
    Red Pepper Sauce 64
    Roasted Red Peppers Stuffed with
        Fennel 128–9
    Watercress and Red Pepper with
        Mascarpone 54–5
pies
    Rhubarb Pie 138–9
    Shepherd's Pie 120–1
Plum Crumble 135
Porcini Sauce 66
'Potato' Pancakes 35
protein 5, 10–11, 14–17, 29, 70
protein powders 16–17, 22, 143–4, 150
pumpkin
    Fried Pumpkin with Deep-Fried Sage
        88–9
    Pumpkin and Goat's Cheese
        Gratin 115
    Spiced Pumpkin, Okra and Baby
        Sweetcorn Casserole 96
Quiche, Swiss Chard 119
Quorn 16, 93

Quick Asparagus, Quorn and Red
    Pepper Stir-fry 99

radicchio 46
    Grilled Fennel with Radicchio and
        Garlic Cream 86–7
radishes 58
    Kohlrabi and Radish Salad 57
Ragoût of Wild Mushrooms 97
Raita, Coriander, Vegetable Curry with
    94–5
raspberries
    Chocolate and Raspberry Layer
        140–1
    Fruit and Flower Compôte in
        Rosehip Tea 133
    Iced Raspberry Shake 27
    Raspberry Coulis 69
    Raspberry and Rose Layer 132
ready-made vegetarian protein 16
Red Pepper Sauce 64
red wine
    Tomato and Red Wine Sauce 62
    Vegetarian Steaks Braised in Red
        Wine 82–3
rhubarb
    Rhubarb Pie 138–9
    Spiced Rhubarb Compôte 139
Rice, Cauliflower, with Thai Curry 98
rice replacements 92, 93, 98
Ricotta and Lemon Pancakes 32
Ricotta Rissoles 87
rose water 132
Rosehip Tea, Fruit and Flower Compôte
    in 133
roulades
    Salad Roulade 50–1
    Spinach Roulade with Mozzarella
        and Tomato Filling 112–13

sage
    Baby Squash with Sage, Cream and
        Gruyère 118
    Fried Pumpkin with Deep-Fried Sage
        88–9
Salad Roulade 50–1
salads 45–58
Salsa, Celery and Tomato 53
sauces 58–69, 90, 103, 125–6
scales 13
seeds 15

seitan 82–3
shakes 22, 27
Shepherd's Pie 120–1
Shortbread, Hazelnut 146
side vegetables 122–9
smoothies 22, 23–5
Sorbet, Vodka and Lemon 131
soups 38–44
Soy Sauce, Sandwiched Tofu with 84
soya 22
soya cream 17
soya flour 143, 144
soya milk 17
soya protein isolate powder 16–17, 143–4,
    150
soya yogurt 14–15
Spaghetti Squash with Dolcelatte Cream
    and Walnuts 104
spinach
    Omelette Cannelloni with Spinach
        Filling 105
    Spinach Roulade with Mozzarella
        and Tomato Filling 112–13
squash
    Baby Squash with Sage, Cream and
        Gruyère 118
    Spaghetti Squash with Dolcelatte
        Cream and Walnuts 104
Steaks, Vegetarian, Braised in Red Wine
    82–3
stevia 18, 19–21, 150–1
Stilton Soup 41
stockists 150–1
storecupboards 14
Strawberry Cheesecake 136–7
Strawberry Smoothie 23
sucralose (Splenda) 18, 19
Swede Soup, Cream of, with Cinnamon
    39
Sweetcorn, Baby, Spiced Pumpkin and
    Okra Casserole 96
sweeteners 18–21
Swiss Chard Quiche 119

Tarragon, Almond and Pecorino Tart 116
tea 22
    Peppermint Tea 28
textured vegetable protein (TVP) 16, 92
Thai Curry with Cauliflower 'Rice' 98
tofu 15
    Mediterranean Tofu Scramble 37

Mockeroni Cheese 108
Sandwiched Tofu with Soy Sauce 84
Spicy Tofu 81
Tofu Chips 78
tomatoes 126
    Celery and Tomato Salsa 53
    Creamy Tomato Sauce 67
    Fennel, Tomato and Black Olive
        Salad 55
    Spinach Roulade with Mozzarella
        and Tomato Filling 112–13
    Stuffed Courgettes with Fresh
        Tomato Sauce 90
    Tomato and Red Wine Sauce 62
    Warm Red Cabbage and Cherry
        Tomato Salad 53
trans-fats (hydrogenated fats) 16
turnips 35, 44, 56–7, 58
    Turnip Gratin Dauphinoise 127

Vegetable Curry with Coriander Raita
    94–5
Vegetable Soup, White, with Paprika
    38, 40
vegetables 9–10, 21
Vegetables, Roasted 129
Vinaigrette 68
Vodka and Lemon Sorbet 131

Waffles, Orange, with Blueberries 34–5
walnuts
    Bitterleaf Salad with Walnut
        Dressing 46
    Spaghetti Squash with Dolcelatte
        Cream and Walnuts 104
watercress
    Chicory, Red Leaf and Watercress
        Salad 49
    Cream of Watercress Soup 44
    Hot Kohlrabi Mash on a Bed of
        Watercress 124
    Watercress and Red Pepper with
        Mascarpone 54–5
weight loss 3
whey powder 151
wine 12

xylitol 19, 131, 151

yogurt 14–15, 132